# Is God Necessary?
## No! and Yes!

By Herbert F. Vetter

Harvard Square Library
*www.harvardsquarelibrary.org*

Designed by Andrew Drane

*Is God Necessary? No! and Yes!*

Published by Harvard Square Library
*www.harvardsquarelibrary.org*

ISBN: 978-0-6151-6046-7

# PREFACE

When I was Director of Student Work at the First Unitarian Church of Chicago in 1950, I organized at the University of Chicago a series of William Ellery Channing Lectures on "Attack and Counterattack in Modern Religion. The opening lecture was by David Riesman, Professor of Sociology and author of *the Lonely Crowd*. The topic was "Freud: Religion as Neurosis."

The crowd was too large for the assigned lecture hall at the Oriental Institute. We tried to move to the university's largest lecture space, Mandel Hall, but an orchestra was playing. When we discovered that the huge Kent Hall science room was available, our guests rushed in and filled all the seats. Then Riesman exclaimed, "Tell them to come back tomorrow night, and I'll speak again." They came and once again filled Kent Hall.

Other lectures in this series critical of religion in the modern world included:

"Marx: Religion in Capitalist Culture"
by James Luther Adams

"Nietzsche: God is Dead"
by Arnold Bergstraesser

"Albert Schweitzer: Opponent of Orthodoxy"
by Leslie Pennington

"Erich Fromm: Humanistic Religion vs. Authoritarian Religion"
by Leslie Pennington

Today there is a new movement critical of religion, "the new atheism" fostered by Daniel Dennett, Richard Dawkins, and Sam Harris. Harris says faith in god or gods is the most dangerous element of modern life, citing Islamic terrorism as well as Judeo-Christianity's growing weapons of mass destruction. Dawkins says the biblical Yahweh is "psychotic," and religion is not only nonsense but a divisive and oppressive force. Dennett describes "the God Delusion" and hopes that practitioners of religion will shrink its maleficent role in civilization.

Is God Necessary? No! and Yes!

The question addressed in this book, *Is God Necessary?*, is not new but is of perennial importance. What is new is that a great new discovery answers this question decisively in the twenty-first century as Darwin's theory of evolution did in the nineteenth century.

H. F. V.

Cambridge, Massachusetts, 2007

# CONTENTS

# PART I

## No! and Yes!

# Is God Necessary?

Is God necessary? As this question has customarily been stated throughout long centuries of philosophical and theological debate, I am compelled to answer in the negative: God is not necessary!

There are several reasons why the answer is negative, and they stem from the fact that the classical idea of God is both an intellectual error and an illusion. God, in this conception, is understood to be outside of space, outside of time, outside of the events which constitute our *daily and enduring* life. If there were such a God, he/she/it would be utterly unknown and unknowable, for the only intelligible assumption for modern people, who live in a world of time-space events, is that any supposed reality outside of actual and possible events in space-time is sheer nothingness. And even if we assume that there is such a reality, it can be of no significance to us earth dwellers, us time- and space-bound creatures, for the simple, common sense reason that we are so constituted as to have no means of apprehending such an other-worldly, utterly static deity. Such a God is, at best, an oblong blur—hardly the appropriate object of our complete devotion.

Instead of holding the eternally contrasting poles within our lives and world in creative, complementary togetherness, orthodox theology dogmatically accepts that strand of Greek thought which asserts that the static is superior to the dynamic, order to change, cause to effect, the eternal to the temporal, the passive to the active, the one to the many. This unwarranted dogma, which has been an uneasy and disruptive cornerstone in the structure of both Eastern and Western civilization throughout the centuries, may fairly be adjudged the supreme intellectual error of our common life, the central fallacy that has plagued, and that continues to plague, the growth of culture, society, and personality.

It is precisely this dogma which directs the orthodox toward their dilemma. According to their theology God dwells outside the world of common life; yet they know first-hand in their religious living that a vital, working, healing God must be found within the world. Thus the orthodox take refuge in the idolatrous deification of a person such as the historic Jesus. The illusion and intellectual errors may now be seen for what they are in truth: the helpless allies of desperate idolatry, the foes of freedom, the enemies of faith in humanity, in life, and in God.

The orthodox swing from pole to pole in underlying conflict: from the negative pole of despair regarding the actual world and its future possibilities to the demonic pole of idolatrous authoritarianism. These are the fateful consequences of their dilemma. This is not to say that orthodoxies of whatever sort, "religious" or "secular," are without their virtues; but it is to say that they stand, in essence, on the side of disruption and despair, hierarchical repression of human growth, imbalance, intolerance, and slavery.

For all who adore the holy ground of freedom, the classical idea of God is a snare and a delusion. Its hopeless oscillation between life's eternally necessary poles provides no adequate basis for the integration of our personal religious living, our changing social structures, our culture, our civilization, our world, our God. Such integration stems from a divine dynamic within our lives and beyond, as a pattern of potentialities not yet realized.

Is God necessary? Not if we mean the classical conception of God! David Hume, in his *Dialogues on Natural Religion*, destroyed once and for all this stubbornly persistent and destructive notion. Who can refute his argument? —that if there were a God who had both absolute power and absolute goodness (and this is just what the classical theists assert) then God would have to be the source of the evil which we find within our lives and in our world.

If God has absolute power and absolute goodness, we have no responsibility, cannot be held accountable for any evil that we do, and have no power either to sin or to create the structures of enduring goodness. If God has absolute power and absolute goodness, then our lives—even at their very best—can contribute nothing whatsoever to the divine life, for, already God has everything needful. Our choices can mean nothing to One who remotely dwells apart from us, containing every whit of unshared power and every trace of goodness. Our suffering can never stir a God who has no passion, no pain, no tragic aspect—only bliss. This is the logic of classical theism, the logic of benevolent despotism. Its God is a tyrant, its kingdom a supremely rigid paternalistic theocracy. Is this God necessary? Not for free, rational people! Yet how pervasive is this root ideological fallacy.

How prevalent, even today, is the tragedy of this error, and the religious depth of this tragedy discloses the sickness of soul. This hollow notion divides the soul in many different ways. It brings continuing clashes between the sciences, philosophy, theology—providing no principle of integration that is consistent with our advancing knowledge of the concrete world in which we live and move and have our being. It creates conflicts of feeling, promoting not only intellectual and emotional discord with the world of fact but also deep attachment for the oblong blur and idols. It seeks, consciously and unconsciously, to destroy our freedom, our choice between alternatives, and our strength of will. Because—with self-righteous piety—it assumes that the standards by which we discern, select, and act are immutably decreed by this absolutely perfect Being and it allows for no variation as life and time advance upon their way. Here is the fallacious logic laid bare: God cannot change in any sense: the altogether changeless One has disclosed (through some deified mediator and some sacrosanct priestly caste) the eternal patterns of perfection which are to determine our choices in particular situations; therefore, all we must do is to submit, and then we will be rewarded, personally, in a beatific world beyond the grave.

These enduring conflicts in the modern soul must be healed if we would move toward health and growth. For long periods, in ancient, medieval, and modern times, Western civilization has been able to function, sometimes with astonishing success, within this essentially clashing framework—much the same as it has been able to endure and to create amidst dreaded outward wars and revolutions. Yet conflict has its breaking point; and oftentimes, at this mid-point in the twentieth century C.E., strife—both outward in the universal war and inward in universal turmoil—is tending toward the goal of sheer annihilation, unless the wounds are healed, the conflicts moderated, and the grace of God restored to humanity in living, sympathetic wholeness.

We must face this fact: neither the orthodox religionists, who must confront the fateful consequences of the classical idea of God which they would promulgate, nor the orthodox secularists who would reject all gods and place their fundamental trust in some new or established social order, can truly meet the demands upon us for redemption. Their souls, now torn, must find a healing touch before they have the truth and power to lead us to a destination other than the City of Destruction. Therefore in terms of the classical idea of God, the answer must be negative: God is not necessary.

But let us ask the question again, this time rephrasing it. Instead of asking, "Is God necessary?" why not ask, "What kind of God is necessary—for adequate human living, for our common task of reconstruction, for the integration of life's poles in persons, peoples, cultures, worlds?" We have a choice: to live or not to live for whatsoever God is True and Beautiful, Just and Whole. In fact, each person must choose, and each must meet the consequence of that decision. We live upon a boundary of choice and consequence. No one escapes—not really! God's balance-wheel is true, precise, and powerful; it is the wheel of Justice and of Law. But what is, who is, this God whom we adore—else we perish? God is that Reality which is truly of ultimate and of sovereign worth, the inescapable Power standing in solemn, sympathetic majesty above the petty gods we fashion with our hands, our hearts, our minds, and our souls. Here is the God above gods, mightier than the mightiest—and yet with limitations on divine powers, providing us with freedom. Here is the God who, with firmness, seeks the integrated growth of life. Here is the Reality each of us meets in all of our experience. Beneath these symbols of divinity lies the reality: dim but unmistakable, distant throughout all time and space but present in each act of every creature. Unclear though our vision be, we still can see that God has a double face, displaying the tortured mask of tragedy as well as the laughing mask of sheer delight. God, with this double face, stands under and above our shells, our walls that hide us from our deeper selves. Living and feeling with our suffering, the weakness and divisiveness within the total person and the total culture, having a craving for togetherness, for growing synthesis of life with life, God—so understood—is the sovereign reality within and behind and yet beyond all our experience. Robert Frost seems to have met this unifying Strength while "mending wall" and has offered a fresh reflection upon the discovery in a poem of that name:

> Something there is that doest love a wall
> That sends the frozen-ground-swell under it
> And spills the upper boulders in the sun;
> And makes gaps even two can pass abreast....

I am convinced that the "Something that doesn't love a wall" is

God, God the Perennial Destroyer of our patterns of exclusive preten-tiousness, our insulating, isolating apathy, our rigid impositions: our demand for conformity to *our* values, *our* preferences, *our* way of do-ing things. That "Something" is God the Wall Destroyer, the Breaker of restrictive boundaries between groups; the Puncturer of our damn-ing, desperate, proud idolatries of race and nation, sect and self. The true God, even the God of Love, is the Leveler of pretensions, the Overturner of our lust for sacred idols of infallibility. This working is one piece with God's creative passion: the fascination for the growing process, the ever-present push toward health and wholeness, the sacred lure toward distant goals—as yet unrealized.

God is that reality which is of ultimate, integral, sovereign worth; and whether it be the creative, sustaining, redeeming or leveling work within our lives and times, this universal Becoming Being is operative. This reality is the God of the scientist, who frames, corrects, rejects hypotheses about the ways of people and things, seeking always for the exact equation between what is in fact and the theory about the fact. This is the God of the sculptor, the architect, the poet, the composer, the dancer; the artists who are given inspiration to fashion forms of beauty for delight, for expression of their new found meanings, and for relating self and others to that which matters most. This is the God of the mother, who expresses in her fond maternal care the genuine con-cern of God for all the creatures, and who, with her partner, joins the sacred common quest for joy, for liberation, for life in more abundance; who establishes and maintains ordered ways of living. This is the God of the business leader, known as wrath in the pursuit of money first and foremost; yet also known as love when freely serving a common good inclusive of self-interest, yet stretching far beyond it. This is the God of the engineer, who builds out of concrete, stone, iron, wood, configura-tions of security and comfort according to our need and nature's laws. This is the God of the teacher, for reality is the teacher of us all; and the one who best teaches youth, teaches both facts and meanings of the facts—stimulating thought, imagination and prompt decision for the better ways, whatever they may be. This is the God of the priest, the rabbi, the minister, when they are faithful to the solemn trust in their possession of making clear to us the working power of God in all we do and feel and think. This is the God of the philosopher and theologian if they truly, freshly seek to comprehend the broader and the broadest factors in our existence, making intelligible these wider generalities through the discipline of reason. Then they disclose the nature of reality, the world, the truly worthful and worshipful. They help us grasp these elemental meanings in the drama of our daily lives.

This is the God that people have loved throughout the ages. This is the God of free faith. Here is the valid object of our reverent search for truth and beauty, justice and integrity. This is the Power of Wholeness we love when we will to live and will to grow. This is the God we dread when we will to thwart the growth of value in the world. Here is the God of all religious experience; that is to say, of all our experience that stretches toward fulfillment, toward deeper harmony of life with life. For the most part it has not been the conceptual God of the philosophers and theologians, but is becoming somewhat more so today. The Einstein of religious thought is the internationally esteemed philosopher and scientist, Charles Hartshorne. Hartshorne opens vistas of the new theism which draws directly upon and squares well with immediate experience, with the methods and findings of the contemporary natural and social sciences, with the insights into reality by our more discerning artists, with the wisdom of reformers, statesmen, prophets, seers—and with the calm demands of common sense. The logic of the new theism is a logic growing out of life and returning back unto the same. It is not the logic of divine despotism but the logic of love. The new theism provides a firm, dynamic center for both stability and change in our ever constant quest for merging life with life at greater height and depth and breadth and in greater strength.

What we have been asserting is that there are two types of belief in God one explicit, the other implicit. Our quarrel here is with the explicit classical idea of God but not with the authentic implicit faith and devotion of people in all periods of human existence when they have perceived that which is truly of sovereign worth. Religious experience is one thing, theology another; just as life and thought are, to some extent, capable of separation. Even so, life cannot be lived with joy and adequacy unless its rudder finds its guide in correct ideas; and thought is meaningless unless it ascends from life and descends unto its source.

Part of the genius of liberal religion is that it does not require intellectual assent to any proposition, even the proposition that God is necessary. For this reason there are within our ranks many noble women and men who justifiably reject the dominant classical idea of God and who are alert to the havoc wrought by this idea. Such folks are citadels of free community, of free religious community. We need them! They are gadflies who sting our indolence and force profound, precise thinking. They adore with their lives the very God whom we adore, even if they choose not to affirm God's name. Words are important—but not essential! Integrity of faith is important—and essential!

Let us now as our question once again, "Is God necessary?" Or shall we ask, "Is Life necessary" The questions are ultimately one and the same.

## The New Atheists

Today there is a new movement radically critical of religion called "the new atheism" featuring Daniel Dennett, Richard Dawkins, and Sam Harris. Harris says faith in God or gods is the most dangerous element of modern life, citing Islamic terrorism as well as Judeo-Christianity's growing weapons of mass destruction. Dennett rejects "religions as social systems whose participants avow belief in a social supernatural agent or agents whose approval is to be sought." Dawkins describes "the God of Delusion" and hopes that practitioners of religion will shrink its maleficent role in civilization.

While a truly lively case can be made that the worst enemy of religion is religion, and the new atheists do have a vital social contribution to make, one almost has to applaud with a single hand since the triple attack relates almost exclusively to supernatural modes of faith.

Consider the ablest of the cooperating trio, **Richard Dawkins**, the distinguished evolutionary biologist who teaches in the United Kingdom at Oxford University. He loves to debate his foes. Raised an Anglican, he began to doubt the existence of God when he was nine years old, and he is now known as the nearest thing to a professional atheist since Bertrand Russell. Dawkins delights in demolishing enshrined musty myths of the Church of England as well as deadly deeds of Islamic terrorism. *The God Delusion* by Dawkins is supplemented by his documentary television broadcasts against religion titled "*The Root of All Evil?*" *Time* magazine celebrated Dawkins as one of the most influential persons in the world in 2007. Nevertheless, I prefer not to exalt this natural scientist who ignorantly exclaims, "If all the achievements of theologians were wiped out tomorrow, would anyone notice the difference?" He dares to add this absurdity: "Even the bad achievements of scientists, the bombs . . . work!"

Dawkins dares to articulate the following God Hypothesis: "There exists a superhuman, supernatural intelligence who deliberately designed and created the universe and everything in it, including us." That hypothesis, which Dawkins names "The God Delusion," is a myth of popular religion which has *not* been endorsed by a world galaxy of modern religious thinkers including Albert Schweitzer, Martin Buber, Sarvepalli Radhakrishnan, Mohammad Iqbal, Albert Einstein, Alfred North Whitehead, and Charles Hartshorne. Therefore, I conclude that Richard Dawkins, the scientist, lacks an adequate working hypothesis for his supposedly devastating attack on God.

Another "new atheist," **Daniel Dennett,** wrote a critique of religion titled *Breaking the Spell: Religion as a Natural Phenomenon.* This eminent professor at Tufts University seeks to eliminate God merely by presenting a limited definition of God; he declares, I repeat, that religions are "social systems whose participants avow belief in a supernatural agent or agents whose approval is to be sought."

When I discovered Dennett's elimination of God by definition on page nine of the first chapter of this 448-page book, I asked myself if I should continue reading a document written by a professor of philosophy who explicitly avoids dialogue with the eminent philosophers of religion of the past century. Dennett's published atheistic identity strikes me as a fight against superannuated supernaturalism and a flight from examining the great modern visions of God. Nevertheless, I found reason to rejoice on page 245 where Dennett quotes his earlier book, *Darwin's Dangerous Idea,* as follows:

> "Is something sacred? Yes, I say with Nietzsche. I could not
> pray to it, but I can stand in affirmation of its magnificence.
> The world is sacred."

It is necessary to underline this affirmation. This new atheist, Daniel Dennett, is also a new theist—a cosmic theist—even though he personally chooses not to use that name.

The third of the new atheists, **Sam Harris**, is a doctoral student in neuroscience who received an earlier degree in philosophy from Stanford University. His first book, *The End of Faith: Religion, Terror, and the Future of Reason* was a *New York Times* bestseller. His thesis is that belief in God is the greatest threat to world peace. Harris is also disturbed by a Gallup poll revealing that 53 percent of Americans are Biblical creationists who do not accept the theory of evolution. He is alarmed about the scientific ignorance of Americans, but I am alarmed that he appears in print to be ignorant of notable views of God that are consistent with science.

The second book by Sam Harris, *Letter to a Christian Nation,* focuses his criticism on Christians who believe that "the Bible is the inspired word of God and that only those who accept the divinity of Christ will experience life after death." Harris says his case is directed against 150 million—"Catholics, mainline Protestants, Evangelicals, Baptists, Pentecostals, Jehovah's Witnesses, and so on."

While this charge is compelling, the Harris case against a Christian nation is confusing. Why does this self-proclaimed atheist simply ignore the notable American liberal Christians such as John Adams, author of the Constitution of the United States; Abigail Adams, the First Lady of one president and mother of another; Thomas Jefferson, author of the Declaration of Independence; Roger Williams, religious liberty pioneer; to say nothing of Ralph Waldo Emerson, Margaret Fuller, Louisa May Alcott, William Ellery Channing, Elizabeth Cady Stanton, Susan B. Anthony, and almost all of the presidents of Harvard College since 1636 A.D.? The polemic of Harris is a fascinating but radically misleading interpretation of the American religious situation.

In sum, though the three "new atheists" often publicly support one another, they do not even try to respond to the new vision of God expressed, for example, by American process philosophers such as Charles Sanders Peirce, William James, Alfred North Whitehead, Charles Hartshorne, and John E. Smith. Although a new epoch of religious thought has arrived, Harris presents no adequate case to defend his new atheism. Dennett offers no case at all against these able modern theists, even though he himself affirms, "The world is sacred." Dawkins joyfully demolishes his native religious home, the Church of England, mistakenly assuming that he has killed God, the Great Delusion.

What a pity! A renaissance of thought comparable to Darwin's theory of evolution and Einstein's theory of relativity has arrived, but the new atheists fail to explicate and celebrate the great new discovery of God due to their compelling preoccupation—denouncing the weary old supernatural God whose death Nietzsche announced in the long gone decades of nineteenth century. Alas!

# Religion's Worst Enemy

In Martin Luther's battle hymn of the Reformation are these words of fighting faith:

> Still our ancient foe
> Doth seek to work us woe.
> His craft and power are great;
> And, armed with cruel hate,
> On earth is not his equal.

The words are strange with power. But what is, who is this ancient foe? Who is this enemy of faith? What is the worst enemy of religion in the modern world?

Is the worst enemy of religion pride? Is it that haughty, classic weasel in the soul, renowned for thriving on and driving toward destruction by tearing down others' personalities so that one's own self-esteem may be exalted to new heights? Is it pride of intellect? pride of property, such as the home in which one lives? pride of family, whether ancestral or contemporary? pride of position, or occupation, of status in the community?

Or is the worst enemy of religion selfishness, the selfishness from which this spirit of arrogance flows? Is it the selfishness that would center all life in one's own person, regardless of the cost to other people—the selfishness that is the untamed fountain of anger and hatred, envy and lust for power, falsehood and greed? Is that the worst enemy of religion?

Or is the enemy of enemies not so much personal as social? Is the worst enemy of religion today nationalism—that passionate attachment to one's own country which blinds one to the need and hopes of other nations? Is it that idolatrous devotion to one's native land which now deadlocks the world in parochial strife?

Or is it racism—that radical denial of the brotherhood of man which again and again erupts to plague the conscience of modern man, dividing mankind according to the ridiculous standard of skin pigment?

Or is it modern war, that puncturer of our pretense to love—the modern war of total populations, by total populations, against total populations? Is total war, war for total stakes, the worst enemy of religion?

As I have reflected on this question, I have been driven toward the conclusion that the worst enemy of religion is not any of these particular personal or social evils, but something which is at once more ultimate and more inclusive—the source from which pride, selfishness, nationalism, racism and war forever grow. I suggest that the worst enemy of religion is religion. As so often happens, the corruption of the best yields the worst. It is not without reason, then, that Paul Tillich, the most creative systematic theologian recently at work in America, declared: "The first word of religion is the word against religion." One might well add that the first word of theology is the word against theology.

This thesis, that the worst enemy of religion is religion, swings sharply counter to the main currents of our time, for today religion is all too effectively exempt from criticism. "You must have faith!" we are repeatedly told, as if faith in faith were sufficient to redeem us from destruction. In view of the contemporary resurgence of religious interest, it is particularly important that certain questions be posed—and answered—without evasion, questions about contemporary religion:

> What is the most segregated hour of the week? Eleven A.M.
> each Sunday morning.
>
> On which area of the earth has more blood been shed than
> anywhere else? The Holy Land.
>
> What institution in the modern world most rigidly adheres
> to irrelevant patterns of the past? The church.
>
> What branch of modern knowledge is the most provincial
> in its basic attitudes and assumptions? I fear it is my own
> branch, theology.
>
> What aspect of our culture has contributed the most to un-
> realistic ethics and the irresponsibility of other-worldliness?
> Religion.

In the face of such questions and their all-too-painful answers, can we defend religion's exemption from criticism? Prophetic religion ever must say *No!* The first word of religion is indeed the word against religion. Has not religion a responsibility to speak the word against its enemy of enemies, religion?

There is more, ever more documentary evidence before us, even in the Bible itself. In the Old Testament, the height of ethical religion was attained by the prophets, who sent the thrust of their attacks against the false religion of their day. Listen to the words of Isaiah:

> What to me is the multitude of your sacrifices? Says the Lord.... Bring no more vain offerings.... I cannot endure iniquity and solemn assembly. Your new moons and your appointed feasts my soul hates; they have become a burden to me, I am weary of bearing them. When you spread forth your hands, I will hide my eyes from you; even though you make many prayers, I will not listen; your hands are full of blood. [Isaiah 1: 11-15; *RSV*]

Consider the life and teachings of Jesus of Nazareth, who stood heroically in the line of the Hebrew prophets. Were not his harshest words spoken against the religious leaders of his own day? One of his disciples left us this invigorating record of a decisive event and address:

> While he was speaking, a Pharisee asked him to dine with him; so he went in and sat at the table. The Pharisee was astonished to see that he did not first wash before dinner. And the Lord said to him, "Now you Pharisees cleanse the outside of the cup and of the dish, but inside you are full of extortion and wickedness. You fools! Did not he who made the outside make the inside also? But give for alms those things which are within; and behold, everything is clean for you.
>
> "But woe to you Pharisees! for you tithe mint and rue and every herb, and neglect justice and the love of God; these you ought to have done, without neglecting the others. Woe to you Pharisees! for you love the best seat in the synagogues and salutations in the market places. Woe to you! for you are like graves which are not seen, and men walk over them without knowing it." [Luke 11: 37-44; *RSV*]

Prophetic religion, in contrast to the religion of mere amiability, has ever in diverse ways cried out: "Beware of the clergy!" My own first word as one who seeks to live a religious life must ever be a word against religion's worst enemy, religion. My first word as a clergyman must be a word against the clergy, of which I am one. When Billy Graham brought his crusade of archaic fundamentalism into New York City, the Protestant clergy of almost all denominations, large and small, joined the bandwagon to support his cause. Protestant clergy of all persuasions graced the platform of piety. Radical questions about the validity of Graham's streamlined yet old-fashioned revivalism were deemed out of order. In America's major metropolis, the Protestant clergy closed ranks in a crusade whose victory, said *The Christian Century*, a vigorous, nondenominational Protestant weekly, would set American religion back more than fifty years. Apart from Reinhold Niebuhr and the *Century*, one could find very few outspoken, independent critics of the Graham crusade.

This situation was not atypical. *Be positive, eternally positive*, say the clergy and the people. How many Americans have ever heard a sermon which spoke in praise of doubt? An all-too-common maxim of the clergy is: leave your doubts in the study when you enter the pulpit. As if their hearers could not bear to hear the truth! As if the congregation needed to take refuge in traditional illusions—in a lazy, meandering faith which refuses to grapple with the doubts of modern man. Across the pulpits of America three words are written in a bloodless, invisible ink: PROPHETS NOT WANTED.

Some years ago, Thomas Jefferson noted the lethargy of the clergy in moving beyond the status quo toward an actual democracy. On the basis of his experience and observation, he concluded that "the clergy, by getting themselves established by law and engrafted into the machine of government, have been a very formidable engine against the civil and religious rights of man." Alexander Hamilton wrote, with reference to the established churches: "What influences in fact have ecclesiastical establishments had on Civil Society? In some instances they have been seen to erect a spiritual tyranny on the ruins of Civil Authority: in many instances they have been seen upholding the thrones of political tyranny; in no instance have they been seen the guardians of the liberties of the people."

Almost alone among the churches, the liberal religious heritage has not brimmed with affirmation devoid of the critical temper. Without a full and freely flowing measure of the courage to doubt, the liberal movement in religion would never have sprung into being. As heirs of the Protestant spirit, we have kept the edge of rational and prophetic criticism carefully honed. Although the burning stake was his lot, Michael Servetus was not afraid to declare his honest doubts. In writing *On the Errors of the Trinity*, he observed:

> How much this tradition of the Trinity has, alas! been a laughing-stock to the Mohammedans, only God knows. The Jews also shrink from giving adherence to this fancy of ours, and laugh at our foolishness about the Trinity.... And not only Mohammedans and Hebrews, but the very beasts of the field, would make fun of us did they grasp our fantastical notion, for all the works of the Lord bless the one God.

If we turn to the most notable champions of the liberal religious outlook in this country, we find the same awareness of faith's deep demand for doubt. William Ellery Channing, in his discourse on "Spiritual Freedom," gave ample recognition of the positive power of religion, interpreting it as "the mightiest agent in human affairs," to which "belongs pre-eminently the work of freeing and elevating the mind." At the same time, Channing noted that;

> Intolerance always shelters itself under the name and garb of religious zeal.... Let religion be seized on by individuals or sects, as their special province; let them clothe themselves with God's prerogative of judgment; let them succeed in enforcing their creed by penalties of law or penalties of opinion; let them succeed in fixing a brand on virtuous men, whose only crime is free investigation; and religion becomes the most blighting tyranny which can establish itself over the mind.

The worst enemy of religion is religion, and an obligation is laid upon us to meet and to rout this enemy. How can this be done?

The first obligation of free men and women is to exercise the courage to doubt. Here is strange doctrine indeed! Religion, we are told, is defense of faith. I would suggest, however, that doubt is faith's hidden affirmation. The women and men of noblest faith have been those of strongest doubt. Out of Gautama's doubts about the prevailing Hinduism of his day has sprung one of our major world faiths, Buddhism. Out of the doubts of Socrates emerged the vital intellectual force of Western civilization. Out of the doubts of Jesus about the established religion of his day came both his crucifixion and the Christian faith. Out of the doubts of Luther arose Protestantism's fighting faith. Out of the doubts of Freud and Nietzsche, Kierkegaard and Whitehead is coming now a New Reformation in religion, a New Reformation open to the demands of world civilization. Forever out of doubt grows faith.

In such a setting, then, we need not only the classical emphasis of the Epistle of James concerning faith and works; we need also a new fusion—of faith and doubt. Modern man's will to believe is twisted out of shape unless it is tempered by the courage to doubt. Doubt is the modern citadel of freedom, standing in eternal opposition to tyranny's idols of infallibility. Courage to doubt is free faith's vital center. Whosoever would be fully human must be a doubter. Encounter with doubt is eternally the price of honest faith. Whoever would ascend to the heights of creative living must first pass through the valley of the shadow of doubt. Capacity for doubt is a measure of humanhood. Ability to doubt is one of the surest guarantees of mature faith.

Out of modern doubt concerning sacred idols of infallibility arose faith in individual freedom of belief as the living center of a responsibly concerned community.

Out of modern doubt concerning walls which thwart the growth of life—walls of national prejudice and pride, of religious exclusiveness, of racial arrogance, of vindictive caste and class—emerged the stand for unrestricted use of reason in religion as the guiding, discipling agent of faith that makes us free and whole, members one of another in a world community of life.

Out of modern doubt concerning every form of tyranny over the mind and body, heart and soul has come faith in generous tolerance of differing religious views and practices within a context of commitment to the democratic process in church and state, school and industry and home.

Out of modern doubt concerning the superstitions, bigotry and idolatry of particular religions comes now a growing faith in Life, uniting people of diverse faiths everywhere in sacred common quest of "truth for the mind; good works for the hands; love for the heart; and for the soul, that aspiring after perfection...which, like lightning in the clouds, shines brightest when elsewhere it is most dark."

16

The courage to doubt is the nerve of freedom and of freedom's faith. The wisdom of doubt is a prelude to faith. The courage to doubt is eternally essential if the church is not to surrender to barbarism but is to serve the Kingdom of God with undiluted strength of heart and hand, mind, and soul. In our warfare against religion's worst enemy—the enemy who incorporates the life-destroying forces of pride, selfishness, nationalism, war, racism and tyranny—we deeply need the courage to doubt. Only thus can our faith be manifest with powerful relevance in the modern world.

# The Church Outside the Church

Just before I talked with him, a provocative young professor who considers himself to be an atheist had been reading Thomas Merton's *The Seven Storey Mountain.* This assignment, an unpleasant discipline for this particular professor, was undertaken as a means of gaining insight into the life of a contemporary man who swung from a Communist orientation to a Roman Catholic orientation, in fact to life in a Trappist monastery.

Why was this autobiography so nauseous to this person, who has been outstanding both for his active defense of American civil liberties and for sacrificial participation in the American labor movement? Primary causes of distaste were Merton s naiveté and his ready surrender of independent judgment. To the professor, this autobiographer s solutions to major problems were and are incredibly simple. In his earlier phase when a young Communist, he regarded capitalism as the cause of every ill; therefore, capitalism must be overthrown, replaced temporarily by the dictatorship of the proletariat, and then be followed by the ultimate bliss of the classless society where there will be no state, no greed, no unhappiness. Next Merton, as a Catholic, repeatedly stated that the supernatural Church is the only true guide, and heaven the reward. For Father Merton, in the Roman Catholic Church there is solace. How clear the doctrine is, and how magnificently it is supported by the force of Scripture and through centuries of a unified, continuous, and consistent tradition. Only through supernatural revelation and divine miracles can one rightly understand. As the ego is surrendered, as one is obedient, superlative joy is known. At last there is relief from the troubles and worries of life in the world. Thus it is the autobiographer's servility to the church which irritates this freedom-conscious social scientist. Particularly disgusting to him are the lines in which Thomas Merton indicated that there is something eminently satisfying in the thought that all Roman Catholics know exactly what they believe, and know what to teach, and all teach the same thing, and teach it with coordination and purpose and great effect.

If this is what religion is, the skeptic might well say, then Marx and Freud are right: religion is an opiate and promotes neuroses. In such a situation, religious liberals will very likely find themselves in substantial agreement with the skeptic. He is our ally in the struggle

18

against theological magic and ecclesiastical absolutism. Moreover, the skeptic often makes excellent criticisms of our own religious ideas and practices.

The severest critics of organized religion can perform an indispensable service because persons within the church all too often fail to see the social and cultural consequences of their faith. Those who are on the "inside" automatically associate church activities with that which is holy, that which is uniquely precious. Thus corporate interest may mask such features as the class bias of certain religious concerns, the use of the church as a vehicle for upward social mobility and for the unconscious or conscious quest for noncommunal personal power. Such motivating factors protrude so that worthy skeptical observers may discern the pretensions of the faithful and, therefore, scorn "the holy" as a perversity to be avoided or opposed.

Let us not be unduly hasty in our condemnation of the self-styled atheist or agnostic, for in these ranks stand many authentic saints—not "abortive saints," as Jacques Maritain would say, but authentic saints, skeptic saints—women and men who are truly committed to God even though they choose not to affirm God's reality. God speaks not only through those who affirm the divine existence but also through those who theoretically deny God. To reverse an old distinction we may speak not only of the *ekklesiola in ekklesia*, the little church within the church, but also of *ekklesia extra ekklesiam*, the church outside the church. No small percentage of the persons who are actively and responsibly laboring for social justice and international peace are still outside the ranks of organized religion, but they are none the less members of the invisible church, the open fellowship of authentic religious search and commitment. Ignazio Silone put the insight cryptically: *They who have gone out of the temple none the less carry within themselves the truth of Christ.*

In this church outside the church may be found the skeptics who launch attack after attack against the forces which would tame the world with monotonous and stifling uniformity, who courageously defend the right of the individual to think freely in every field of inquiry, who unseat the mighty who rule without consent or without allowing civil freedoms, who reject sad-faced, world- withdrawing piety and find humor and vitality consistent with the highest good. Those who are skeptical of the popular gods or prevalent religious practices are part of the vanguard of opposition to the evils of our time, refusing to bend the knee before the idols of rigid ecclesiasticism, militant nationalism, human pretentiousness, dogmatic finality, and illusory supernaturalism.

Moreover, the history of the modern mind is in large measure a history of skepticism. Philosophy has assumed the role of rebel in its reaction against domination by the medieval queen of the sciences, revealed theology. Through gaining its autonomy philosophy has made vigorously critical and constructive strides through such doubters as Bacon and Descartes, Spinoza and Hume, Locke and Mill, James and Dewey, Whitehead and Hartshorne.

Modern insistence upon the autonomy of the natural and social sciences has likewise immeasurably promoted the advancement of knowledge, an advancement which has been won only through warfare against fortresses of faith. Galileo, Newton, Darwin, Freud: each fought intensely against strongholds of devout ignorance. Even in politics the struggle has been as much that of doubt as of faith, of unbelief as of belief. In the pageant of democracy the leaders have often been regarded as skeptics, if not infidels: Voltaire, Paine, Jefferson, Franklin, Holmes. These are leaders who have warred against idolatries which stifle the democratic spirit.

Then let us praise God for skeptics, skeptics who have rejected the flight to a security that throttles creativity, who have refused to permit divine theology to be enthroned as radically superior to the disciplines of science and philosophy, who deny that any idea, or book, or person, or state, or church is so holy, so perfect, as to be exempt from the challenge of criticism. The skeptic is a whip that stirs a complacent humanity to alert thought, consistent action, and fresh creation. No longer can bovine souls languish in an abyss of mediocrity, nor can the wielder of power pursue an unjust path without prophetic rebuke and organized opposition.

Skepticism is a citadel of free community, respecting human beings as brothers and sisters, rejecting inner certitude when there is no outward certainty. Let us not fear the skeptic nearly so much as the naïve believer. The atheist is usually insistent upon leaving the door of free inquiry ajar, whereas the believer, in his or her divine certitude, too often readily slams it shut. Thus the atheist often is actually on our side, for free inquiry is indigenously liberal religious in its essence, and adherence to any particular theory or article of belief is secondary at most, even though that theory or belief pertains to God.

Therefore, we speak in praise of skepticism, despite the fact that skepticism is not enough. Life demands not only the defense, the citadel, which skepticism provides but, above all, high levels of creative affirmation. The citadel will serve to repel the attackers of free community, but positive motive power is requisite also. Doubt, like faith itself, is of but partial validity. Every doubt implies belief; every denial of God which is not a denial of the value of life itself is an affirmation of divinity. The issue is never between God or no God but rather between this God or that God; there is some ultimate object of faith and devotion, however unorthodox it may be.

Even science, which is preeminently tough-minded and tough-souled, has its affirmations. The cornerstone of modern science is compounded of both cautious skepticism and cautious faith; skepticism regarding the intrusion of the divine from a world outside space-time, but faith in the fundamental orderliness of the universe; skepticism regarding our easy lapse into the pit of dogmatic certainty, yet faith in the possibility of humanity's achieving greater knowledge of actual and possible events; skepticism regarding authoritarian methods of inquiry, but faith in the free cooperative endeavors of people searching for truth and knowledge and testing their hypotheses and basic principles with reason and observation. Thus both affirmation and negation are ever present.

Viewed in this context, we might liken the function of the skeptic to the checks and balances of democratic government. The skeptic, by opposing every endeavor directed toward clutching the divine in a book, person, or institution, forces a partition of powers, not allowing any group to become so powerful that it can crush those persons who disagree. No claim of infallibility rides unchecked, and no monopolization of power by the God-hoarders is likely where healthy doubt survives. The very negation of the skeptic is a defense against pretentious faith and religious intolerance. Nevertheless, just as democratic checks are not instruments of positive activity, so doubt is a citadel of free community which must be balanced by faith and commitment.

The church outside the church offers its important contribution, but that does not mean that it is without serious weaknesses and dangers. We must persistently ask the skeptics what they regard as supreme if not the God who is Reality. Is the object of devotion to be the self, the nation, the state, or humanity? Then there is no ultimate meaning of life and no enduring basis for moral action. Such gods must perish as all idols perish.

Furthermore, the church outside the church is ever in danger of being religiously irrelevant. Skeptics who condemn all religion because in the past religion has been primarily authoritarian and supernatural overlook promising contemporary developments in religious thought and practice. They fall backwards into the trap of pure traditionalism, thinking only in terms of what has been, not what may be. All too often skeptics actually neglect to consider religion rationally, examining the various possible types of religious experience and orienting themselves in the light of those types which are most meaningful. The point is that no living, sane person can avoid having some effective orientation to ultimate, integral divine reality and of a consequent sense of comparative values. The skeptic is inevitably a religious person of some sort. Thus comes the question, "Is the skeptic's explicit faith worth having?" That question he or she too rarely dares to ask.

Still the church outside the church does have its virtues. As a relativist, the skeptic eternally opposes competing authoritarianisms which do not allow for democratic compromise. For example, liberal religious skeptics will criticize both fundamentalism and Catholicism insofar as they limit academic and civil liberties. Thus they plow fertile ground for free community. At the same time, insofar as they are humanitarian, they are both sympathetic to human inner anxiety and diligent in advocating political action to provide security for the anxious. These are qualities within the church outside the church which appeal to hosts of sophisticated modern men and women. Some of us within the church will deplore these qualities as being part of a trend toward degrading secularization of our culture. Others, aware of serious weaknesses in the ranks of both skeptics and believers, will sense that in many instances *they who have gone out of the temple nonetheless carry within themselves the truth of Christ.*

# Where Is Reliable Power?

An ancient question haunts modern men and women who face facts of both life and death: "Where is your God?"

As we ponder this problem, we may find it helpful in our present situation to rephrase this question dealing with the object of man's authentic faith, asking in the language of secular life: Where is reliable power?

In terms of precise mathematical logic, there are only three possible answers to this question: (1) reliable power is *somewhere*; (2) reliable power is *nowhere*; (3) reliable power is *everywhere*. In our day-to-day actions we are forced to answer our question by giving one of these three possible answers, or some combination of the three. What answer do you give?

Reliable power *somewhere*? For example, do you act as if the power of the sun is reliable? Humanity has always been absolutely dependent upon the sun for survival and fulfillment on this planet. In a single second our sun generates more power than people have used since the beginning of civilization on this planet. Each day streams of fire leap forth from the sun for 50,000 miles. This radiant power has been pouring forth for 5 billion years, and scientists expect this energy to flow for another 5 billion years. Finally, in due time, the sun will likely grow into a monstrous red ball so large that it will engulf its nearest planets: Mercury, Venus, Earth, Mars. From the standpoint of the family of man, therefore, the sun is reliable power, but this affirmation can hardly be the full answer to our question since we know that the finite sun will fail someday. What then shall we conclude?

Is reliable power *nowhere*? When we recall that the sun—which is one of a hundred billion stars in the Milky Way—was born and will die, we realize that it is not worthy of our total trust. In this sense, reliable power is nowhere; it is not somewhere in just a fragment of space-time-power. The thrust of this negation is expressed not only by the scientist but by the artist. Consider "the prophet of Minimal Art," Ad Reinhardt. For years he painted one black square after another, each square being virtually empty of images, empty of positive colors, empty of moving patterns of meaning and value. This art which negates art has been presented at the Museum of Fine Arts and in a *LIFE* feature on Ad Reinhardt, "Master of the Minimal." Such paintings declare:

reliable power is nowhere. Nonetheless, who can live on mere husks of negation? Perhaps we had best turn to our third possibility.

Is reliable power *everywhere*? The fiery sun participates in the deathless drama of power. In terms of the principle of the conservation of energy, nothing is ever lost. The strength of the living-dying sun is preserved in the eternal procession of power, since energy is neither created nor destroyed but is forever transformed from one thing to another, worlds without end. Despite all this, however, who can wisely worship a mere abstraction—even one affirming that reliable power is everywhere?

What then shall we conclude when we ponder the question before us? Whether we listen to the ancient taunt asking, "Where is your God?" or listen to the modern declarations of humanity's hidden faith, we come to the same conclusion: Reliable Power is *somewhere-nowhere-everywhere* always.

# What We Stand For

What are the working principles of socially responsible liberal religion? How do we daily express our faith through our action in today's society? With respect to democracy in America, what is the role of a socially concerned congregation?

There is never any single way to answer such questions, and it is important to note that we are neither the first to raise such issues, nor the first to answer. For generations, those who have gone before us have fashioned working principles of liberal religious living, saying *Yes* to what enhances Life and *No* to all that thwarts movement toward the fullness of life. We are continuing heirs of enduring working principles of socially responsible religion, faithful principles which undergird and overarch our institutions.

1. We stand for individual freedom of inquiry and belief as a vital center of responsibly creative and concerned community.

   Therefore, we stand opposed to every idol of infallibility: Idols of the Book, the Person, the Church, the State, the Tradition—idols meant to have immunity to criticism, idols which forever retard advancing truth by rigid requirements of conformity in faith and life.

2. We stand for unrestricted use of reason in religion as a guiding, disciplining agent of the faith that makes people free and whole, members one of another in an emerging world community of life.

   Therefore, we stand opposed to every wall of antirational devotion which cripples life: Walls of nationalistic prejudice, religious exclusiveness, racial arrogance, and vindictive caste and class.

3. We stand for tolerance of differing religious views and practices within a context of commitment to the democratic process in church and state, school and industry and home.

   Therefore, we swear upon the altar of God eternal hostility to every form of tyranny over the human body, mind, heart, and soul.

4.   We stand for religion as a human experience of what is real, yet waiting to be realized; what is ideal, yet the greatest of present facts; religion as adventure, a flight after the unattainable; religion as integrating encounter with life as it is and life as it can be.

Therefore, we stand eternally opposed to the irreligious force of fragmentary purpose which disregards the religious vision; and, likewise, to every form of faith that surrenders creative zest to stifling uniformity.

5.   We stand for fellowship which is truly ecumenical, embracing east and west and north and south; uniting men and women and children of diversity of faith in sacred common quest for:

*truth for the mind,*
*good works for the hand,*
*love for the heart,*
*and for the soul that aspiring after perfection,*
*that unfaltering faith in Life which, like lightning in the clouds,*
*shines brightest when elsewhere it is most dark.*

# Two Americas: Hemingway and Frost

## Ernest Hemingway

In 1923 Ernest Hemingway gave his sister a copy of his first published book. Removing the dark green paperbound volume from his pocket, he said, "Don't show this to the family!"

*Three Stories and Ten Poems* had been printed in Paris. The respected Dr. Hemingway of suburban Oak Park outside Chicago was spared the agony of ever seeing this book by his son, but he was sent six copies of Ernest's second book, *In Our Time*. Horror-struck by these stories, he neatly wrapped all six and turned grimly toward the post office. Ernest's mother urged that they keep just one copy of their son's first book. Declaring that he would tolerate no such filth in his Christian home, Dr. Hemingway did what he had to do. When his father returned these books to the publisher, Ernest stopped writing to his family.

Later Dr. Hemingway came to appreciate such of his son's works as *The Sun Also Rises*, published in 1926. The mother's doubled-minded attitude toward her son was shared by many other people, but there were those who saw that he had an element which is always essential for greatness in any realm of life: he dared to be himself; he was no copy, Ernest Hemingway was Ernest Hemingway. Whoever wished him to be somebody else would be disappointed. He lived his life distinctively in deeds, and he expressed his life distinctively in words. Even those who may not like the man may appreciate the immense contribution which his earnest life made to life, though that contribution was etched in black.

Ernest Hemingway took life and literature straight. Always writing of the winner who loses and of the final failure of success, Ernest intensely wished to be a champion and seldom felt that he was. He wrote of death. He wrote brightly of those who met death with daring. He wrote darkly of those who met death without daring. He wrote of death because Death was the Enemy. Hemingway knew that nothing else was really worthless. He did not sidestep tragedy. He was fascinated by death. Each story, like his life, was a baptism in blood. The first story in his first full book is about an "Indian Camp" in northern Michigan. Hemingway's hero, Nick Adams, is the son of a doctor. In this particular story, Nick is the young boy who holds the basin while his father delivers a baby by Caesarian section, using only a jacknife, using no anesthetic. The invalid father of the baby has been in the bunk above the mother. For two days he has listened to her screaming. The doctor looks up after the delivery and discovers that the father has almost removed his own head with a razor.

All Hemingway stories were like that. Nick experienced shock, strife, struggle. Nick's father, Dr. Adams, committed suicide. In these stories, Nick Adams conducts himself nobly in the losing battle which is life. Nick is the man of courage Hemingway wished he were. Hemingway was a winning loser: a man of violence against animals, against other humans, against himself. Ernest Hemingway is Santiago, hero of *The Old Man and the Sea*. Having fished for 84 days and caught nothing, he dares to enter the Gulf Stream and catches a giant marlin. Pulled day and night, day and night, the old Cuban fisherman clings to his catch. He kills it with his harpoon and lashes it to his skiff. Then come the sharks. He can kill only so many. The skeleton remains to be towed home. This is the victory. Santiago is the winner who loses in the arena of life as war unto death.

Hemingway, a Nobel Laureate in Literature, was the winner who lost. He went down fighting, losing to himself. His brother spoke truly in saying, "He died as he lived—violently." On July 2, 1961 Ernest fondled his silver inlaid shotgun for the last time. He died alone. Thus he lived his vision of life as slaughter, life as ultimately meaningless struggle, life as existence without God. The open secret is: he shows us what life is when "God is dead."

## Robert Frost

In Boston on January 29, 1963, America's unofficial poet laureate, Robert Frost, died. As was true of another citizen of the world, Ernest Hemingway, uncommonly historic high words of deep appreciation came from the Kremlin and the White House. The Premier's words bespoke the poet's love of the common people and his contribution to our world civilization. The President focused on Frost's universally local qualities: his love of nature, his plain speech, his canny wisdom, his insight into the soul. "He had promises to keep, and miles to go, and now he sleeps."

The poet of freedom knew tragic joy for 88 years. His days were not devoid of tears, though some have thought he was unduly optimistic.

His father died when he was ten. His first son, Eliot, died at four. His daughter, Marjorie, married and then died from a childbirth infection. He lived for 25 years after Mrs. Frost died. Five years after her death their other son, Carole—"who had the seeds of genius in him"—destroyed himself. Another daughter was an invalid. Robert Frost was not unacquainted with sorrow, but he never tried to be a conqueror of nature, nations, or God. He was a person of power. Instead of cursing God, he joked with him. By laughing at himself, he taught us how to trust. Somehow he had a way of ministering by awakening wisdom in us.

Some say his work is rural and leads folk not to seek to solve complex problems, but only to escape from social responsibility. Perhaps that word is something less than altogether fair. It is true that Robert Frost was neither radical nor conservative. I've heard him smile and say,

> *I never cared to be radical when young*
> *For fear it would make me conservative when old.*

Still, he may for all that have been true to life's classic balance wheel. He was a realist who spoke of a star:

> It asks of us a certain height,
> So when at times the mob is swayed
> To carry praise or blame too far,
> We may choose something like a star
> To stay our minds on and be staid.

The star to which he pointed was larger than the eye could ever see. Nevertheless, he himself has been a steady and steadying star which not a few of us have seen at night since we were young. We never learned how not to honor him.

Robert Frost's poetry hides and reveals the classic motto of universal sanity and health: Never too much! His life shows forth a joyful secret: Love Life without reserve; and be not ashamed to be a swinger of birches. Yes, he sold all he possessed to buy one treasure, and his purchase has enriched the world. He put his money on the Power which is somewhere-nowhere-everywhere and endless. He was not afraid to live. He was not afraid to die. He had a "lover's quarrel with the world."

# Beyond All Gods

In terms of conversations within the liberal religious movement now and throughout the twentieth century, a great question before us is: Should the object of our supreme devotion be the human family or should it be the dynamic cosmos of which humanity is but a part? We religious liberals always put high value on both humanity and nature, and today the humanist and theist philosophies of life are once again fashioned in the light of degrees of this double affirmation of devotion. As a religious animal, a human being not only has the intelligence to envision an object of supreme devotion for oneself and for all of humanity; one also does in fact—throughout the processes of health and healing—find forms of integral personal security precisely through such orientation and commitment to some object of ultimate devotion.

Our question is, then, part of a larger question: What is the proper object of our supreme loyalty and love? Let us personalize the question: Should I personally be the primary object of my own devotion? Should my ultimate devotion be given to some concrete other self or group of selves such as my family, my nation, or humanity—in either actual or ideal form. Or should my ultimate object of devotion be that natural divine reality which includes and yet transcends all of these lesser loyalties? Negatively speaking, I should like to state the question this way: Is it not true that if I deify one of these egocentric or ethnocentric gods, I can find no ultimate security, no ultimate meaning of my life, and no enduring basis for moral action? Are not all of these gods, who are less than reality or nature as infinitely lovable, doomed to extinction at some future time? If I devote my life to one of these, will not all meaning and value be lost when the finite object of my devotion perishes? Is not some more valid faith not only religiously available but also pragmatically imperative for the fullest realization of the life of humanity? Thinking that it is, I would present a case for our finding security through a humanistic naturalistic theism which moves beyond all gods and yet is faithful to the freedom which liberal religious living forever requires for its fulfillment.

Faith in ourselves as creative participants in an everliving, ever-changing pluralistic universe at once provides an invaluable check upon perennial human tendencies to lapse into either world fleeing illusions or idolatry. Indeed, is not a basic form of idolatry the adoration of a part as having higher worth than the whole? My thesis is that humanistic naturalistic theism contains all of the positive values of naturalistic humanism but avoids certain of the latter's narrowing negations—especially whenever it repudiates all ideas of God.

First, however, let us recall some of the major areas of agreement between these two forms of naturalism. Both naturalistic humanists and naturalistic theists assert that reality consists of actual and possible events in space-time and the relations between them. Both reject supernaturalism, the assertion that there is something beyond such events in space-time. Both reject the belief that humanity's chief end is to find some personal salvation in another world beyond death. Both reject the traditional theism which asserts that God is an utterly transcendent Being without body and without becoming, a superspatial Being bursting into history from beyond through miraculous action revealing the divine in our mundane world. In addition to rejecting such traditional theism, both also reject the traditional pantheism which affirms the opposing monopolar extreme, a world without change and without chance. These common negations are the consequence of certain vital common affirmations. Both naturalistic humanists and naturalistic theists cherish and promote modern science and root their concepts in its methods, its principles, and its findings. Both share an evolutionary perspective on life.

In presenting a case for humanistic naturalistic theism, I should like to keep close to our actual religious experience, beginning with the operational faith of the scientist. What, in terms of behavior, is the creative natural scientist's actual object of supreme devotion? Is it not devotion to nature, nature not as a mere instrument to be manipulated or used by us but as having meaning and worth in its own right? Consider Darwin's love of the lowly earthworm or Maeterlinck's love of the bee. Such portions of nature are experienced and interpreted by great scientists not as a mere means of human fulfillment but as having intrinsic value. Likewise, consider the astronomer's fascination with the galaxies. Observation of the actual behavior of the scientific observer leads us to think that knowledge of the universe springs quite spontaneously and directly from affection for nature in and of and for itself. There is good reason in the records of the lives of scientists for thinking that such monumental discoveries as those of Copernicus,

31

Kepler, Galileo, and Newton are precious fruits of religious devotion to the cosmos conceived as the embodiment of God.

The natural scientist's religious experience of nature is explicitly expressed when Albert Einstein speaks of cosmic mysticism as the driving force of creative science: "The most beautiful emotion we can experience is the mystical. It is the source of all true art and science. He to whom this emotion is a stranger, who can no longer wonder and stand in awe, is as good as dead. To know that what is impenetrable to us really exists, manifesting itself in the highest wisdom and the most primitive forms—this knowledge, this feeling, is at the center of all true religiousness. The cosmic religious experience is the strongest and the noblest thing behind scientific research which is derived from it."

In the field of ethics, as well as in that of scientific description of empirical knowledge, do we not also most properly make our decisions in terms of a context which is ampler than just human welfare? Are the plant world and the animal world of no real and enduring worth except insofar as they serve the ends of humanity? If this is so, then is not the proper object of our devotion the reality which transcends, as well as includes, us. Humanistic naturalistic theism sees moral action in personal, social, and cultural life in terms of our creative contribution to life, and ultimately to the deathless cosmic Life. We are cocreators with God, and so are all other creatures. The question then arises, do we not agree with Albert Schweitzer when he says: "The more deeply we look into nature, the more we recognize that it is full of life, and the more profoundly we know that all life is a secret and that we are united with all life that is in nature. From this knowledge comes our spiritual relationship to the universe."

Having briefly considered the proper object of our supreme devotion as related to ethics as well as to science, let us now ask: What is the valid object of devotion for the artist? Does not the artist's real religion lie in appreciative awareness of persons as well as of natural objects such as mountains and rivers, trees and birds, as well as the artist's abstraction from the concrete flow of such eventful entities? Do not cosmic dimensions of depth break through notable artistic creations? For example, sometimes naturalistic humanists speak of Beethoven's works as triumphs of the humanistic outlook, and so in a sense they are, but not necessarily to the exclusion of their being pervasively theistic. As Frank Lloyd Wright said in his latter years: "All of my life I have listened to Beethoven as the master architect of all time; the most profound student of Nature known, one whose inspired imaginative resource is beyond comparison. I wish more life to more creative music revealing the cosmic rhythms of great Nature, Nature spelled with a capital N as we spell God with a capital G. Why? Because Nature is all of the body of God we mortals will ever see." In his architecture Wright notably expressed the humanistic naturalisic theism which he liked to define in terms of a principle which he called the Unitarian abstract. The natural house and organic architecture are among the flowerings of this creatively unifying faith.

An ally to this cause is Julian Huxley, the biologist and philosopher of life who preferred not to employ the traditional word "God" to convey his implicitly theistic meaning. Listen to his living words: "The religion of the future must have as its basis the consciousness of sanctity in existence. The experience of the universe as affecting human life—and therefore as invested with sanctity—is the Sacred Reality and is the proper object of religion. Humanity is rooted in what transcends it."

Consider also the case for humanistic naturalistic theism in terms of major needs of our time for the growth of world community and the achievement of integration in our personal religious living. Does not a secure religious foundation for world community lie in the realization of each individual's being a vital cell in the body of humanity, which is a precious portion of the cosmos? Some lines of Norman Cousins sing this theme with invigorating power: "I am a single cell in a body of two billion cells. The body is mankind. I glory in self, but my individuality does not separate me from my universal self, the oneness of mankind. If I deny the oneness of humanity, I deny the oneness of God. Therefore, I affirm both. Without a belief in human unity I am hungry and incomplete. The sense of human unity makes possible a reverence for life. It is a sense of the whole, a capacity for wonder, a respect for the intricate universe of the individual life."

Ponder also this practical question: How can you and I achieve the finest creative integration of our own personalities? I suggest that this may well best be done through the affirmations of humanistic naturalistic theism.

One clue to an answer to this question is visible in these words of a mathematician and philosopher, Alfred North Whitehead, who says:

"God is *in* the world, or nowhere, creating continually in us and around us. This creative principle is everywhere——in the ether, water, earth, and human hearts. Insofar as we partake of this creative process we partake of the divine, of God, and that participation is our immortality, reducing the question of whether one's individuality survives death of the body to the state of an irrelevancy. Our true destiny as cocreator in the universe is our dignity and our grandeur."

# PART II

America's New Vision of God

Is God Necessary? No! and Yes!

# Preface

A new discovery comparable to Darwin's theory of evolution and Einstein's theory of relativity (symbolized by the equation $E = mc^2$) is the theory of power as divine relativity or panentheism developed primarily by a group of amazing American thinkers sometimes known as process philosophers. Among them are Charles Sanders Peirce, William James, William Ernest Hocking, Alfred North Whitehead, and Charles Hartshorne. Here are brief descriptions of them and their bold contributions to a new vision of God which commands celebration.

# Charles Sanders Peirce

In the early 1870s, a small group of young men formed a Harvard Square circle for philosophical discussion. Meeting sometimes in the study of Charles Sanders Peirce and sometimes in the study of William James, they half-ironically, half-defiantly called themselves The Metaphysical Club.

In those youthful Harvard Square philosophical discussions, the doctrine of pragmatism saw the light in 1873. The meaning of an idea could be known only if one considered its consequences for practical experience, for actual or possible action. In writing later to Peirce, William James exclaimed, "There is no more original thinker than yourself in our generation." The two had become acquainted when both of them were studying chemistry in the Lawrence Scientific School. Charles's father, Benjamin Peirce, the Perkins Professor of Mathematics and Astronomy at Harvard, has been described as America's most eminent scientist in the nineteenth century. He was one of the incorporators of the National Academy of Sciences, one of the founders of the Harvard Observatory, and author of *The History of Harvard University 1636-1775*. His students included two future presidents of the university, Charles William Eliot and A. Lawrence Lowell.

Among the familiar figures in the home in which Charles grew up were not only leading men of science such as Louis Agassiz (his father's closest friend) but Margaret Fuller, Judge Story, Henry Wadsworth Longfellow, James Russell Lowell, Daniel Webster, James Freeman Clarke, William Henry Channing, and sometimes Ralph Waldo Emerson. In *The Development of Peirce's Philosophy*, Murray G. Murphey says of Charles's father: "The elder Peirce was a deeply religious man of the Unitarian school. He regarded nature as the exemplar of the wisdom of the Divine Geometer, and science as a means to understanding that wisdom." He affirmed, *There is but one God, and science is the knowledge of God.* This spirit went forth in the son.

Charles Peirce was born in Cambridge in 1839. He learned to read and write without the usual instruction. At the age of eight he fell hopelessly in love. To drown his sorrow, he studied chemistry. His father used to play a card game—double rummy—with him from 10 in the evening until dawn, teaching the child concentration by correcting each mistaken play. While still in high school, the youngster was reading no less a work than Kant's *Critique of Pure Reason*.

When Charles was a student at the Cambridge High and Latin School, however, he played hooky and managed to get himself expelled several times. Nevertheless, he did graduate and went to Harvard College, where he was the first person to receive a Bachelor of Science degree in chemistry *summa cum laude*. Then assisting at the Harvard Observatory, he was given the honor of being asked to deliver a series of Harvard lectures on philosophy. It became clear to him in the Metaphysical Club discussions that, *What a man really believes is what he would be ready to act upon, and to risk much upon.*

In 1877, when Charles was sailing to Europe to attend a scientific conference, he wrote "How to Make Our Ideas Clear"—the classic *Popular Science* paper which to this day marks the origin of a continuing series of publications in which he delineated the philosophy of pragmatism. This article was the foundation work of a theological revolution whose end is nowhere in sight, and whose premise is, I think, possibly second to none within the past century. It is a philosophy of freedom, chance, evolution with respect to personality as well as God. As his frame of thought developed, Charles Sanders Peirce spoke of "firstness," "secondness," and "thirdness."

Let it suffice now to note that here is an evolutionary philosopher who took growth seriously. Here is a man who in the very foundations of his thought put potentiality first as an aspect of reality. His is truly a philosophy of freedom since, even for God, the future is not wholly determined. Here now we have an early inkling of the contribution made by the first of several persons who have helped give us an understanding of the God of our ever open Universe. For a glimpse of America's new vision of God—a science oriented, world-affirming vision—note the power of these words of Charles Sanders Peirce:

> Reference to the future is an essential element of personality. Were the ends of a person already explicit, there would be no room for development, for growth, for life; and consequently there would be no personality. The mere carrying out of predetermined purposes is mechanical. This remark has an application to the philosophy of religion. It is that a genuine evolutionary philosophy, one that makes the principle of growth a primordial element of the universe, is so

far from being antagonistic to the idea of a personal creator that it is really inseparable from that idea.

According to that logical doctrine which the present writer first formulated in 1873 and named Pragmatism, the true meaning of any product of the intellect lies in whatever unitary determination it would impart to practical conduct under any and every conceivable circumstance, supposing such conduct to be guided by reflexion carried to an ultimate limit.

We can know nothing except what we directly experience. So all that we can anyway know relates to experience. Where would such an idea, say as that of God, come from, if not from direct experience? Open your eyes——and your heart, which is also a perceptive organ——and you see God.

Everybody can see that the statement of St. John (God is Love) is the formula of an evolutionary philosophy, which teaches that growth comes only from love, from the ardent impulse to fulfill another's highest impulse. The philosophy we draw from John's gospel is that this is the way mind develops; and as for the cosmos, only so far as it yet is mind, and so has life, is it capable of further evolution. Love, recognizing germs of loveliness in the hateful, gradually warms it to life, and makes it lovely.

# William James

Charles Peirce's best friend, William James, was named for William James of Albany, who emigrated from Ireland about 1789, participated in the opening of the Erie Canal, and accumulated some three million dollars—one of the great fortunes of the time. William James's father, the older Henry James, attended Princeton Theological Seminary, but soon abandoned it and his family's Calvinistic faith. In 1886, the elder Henry James moved from New York City to Cambridge, Massachusetts. He had acquaintance with Emerson beginning about the time of the birth of William James in 1842. Indeed, Emerson proposed the elder Henry James as a charter member of the Saturday Club, which began in 1855-56 at Parker's Hotel in Boston. The original members included Louis Agassiz, Richard Dana, James Russell Lowell, and Benjamin Peirce. After attending the Lawrence Scientific School, where his teacher was Charles W. Eliot, William James attended Harvard Medical School. Soon depression struck, disabling him for almost five years. His friendship with Oliver Wendell Holmes, Jr. was especially important to him at this time. In 1876 his career was secure as a Harvard professor. For more than a decade, he worked on *The Principles of Psychology*, published in 1890. Some of us may remember encountering the striking chapter of that book entitled "Habit." James also published various essays entitled *The Will To Believe*.

His Gifford Lectures delivered in 1900, are a fascinating description of *The Varieties of Religious Experience*. Three years before, he had remarked, "Religion is the great interest of my life." In these lectures, he communicates with boldly intense colors the contrast between the religion of the healthy-minded and the religion of the twiceborn sick soul.

Among his essays, we find one on the question "What Makes a Life Significant?" He answers: struggle, risk, courage—heroism makes life significant. To those who knew him, James himself was truly a hero of the mind. He even dared to affirm that God is finite, struggling, helping others, as well as needing help in the struggle against evil. The Hibbert Lectures by James at Manchester College, Oxford University in 1908, were on *A Pluralistic Universe*. There we find these words expressing this philosopher's vision of God:

God himself may draw vital strength and increase of very

being from our fidelity. I do not know what the sweat and
blood and tragedy of this life may mean, if they mean anything short of this. If this life be not a real fight, in which
something is eternally gained for the universe by success, it
is no better than a game of private theatricals. . . . But it feels
like a real fight—as if there was something really wild in the
universe which we are needed to redeem; and first of all to
redeem our own hearts from atheisms and fears. For such a
half-wild, half-saved universe our nature is adapted.

My thesis is this: Anything short of God is not rational, anything more than God is not possible.

Theism is and will be the centre of gravity for all attempts to
solve the riddle of life. And theism must mean the faith of
that person who believes that God be conceived as the deep-
est power in the universe, a power not ourselves which not
only makes for righteousness, but means it, and which rec-
ognizes us. At a single stroke, theism changes the dead blank
"it" of the world into a living thou, with whom the whole
person may have dealing. We are indeed internal parts of
God.

# William Ernest Hocking

William Ernest Hocking is still another Harvard Square contributor to America's evolving conception of God, a conception which enables us to cope with and relate creatively to reality rather than to retreat to an otherworldly, utterly transcendent God of illusion. Born in Cleveland in 1873, he received his A.B., A.M., and Ph.D. degrees from Harvard. The minister of the First Parish in Cambridge, Unitarian, Samuel McChord Crothers, officiated at his marriage to Agnes Boyle O'Reilly in the home of the bride's father, John Boyle O'Reilly, the Irish-born poet. Richard Hocking, the son of William and Agnes, and a teacher of philosophy in his own right, was one of my own teachers of philosophy at the University of Chicago. When I later presented to him the idea of America's new vision of God to which his father had contributed, he encouraged me to develop these thoughts.

William Ernest Hocking, professor of philosophy at Harvard from 1914 to 1943, except for his service at the front during WWI, was a member of the Society of Mayflower Descendents and the American Society of Puritan Descendents. His publications represent a Puritan-like range of concern. Consider some of the books by him: *The Meaning of God in Human Experience, Human Nature and Its Remaking, The Lasting Elements of Individualism, Rethinking Missions, Types of Philosophy, A Free and Responsible Press, Science and the Idea of God, The Coming World Civilization, The Meaning of Immortality in Human Experience.*

In 1960 it was my privilege during annual meetings of the American Unitarian Association to introduce Dr. Hocking when he delivered, in the Harvard Square Meeting House of the First Parish in Cambridge, the inaugural address in an annual series entitled the Colloquium on God and the Modern World. Hocking, then 86, spoke with the vigor of a commander-in-chief of ideas. Note how he meets head on the major doubts of the modern scientific mind in the following words:

> The "Modern World" is a distinct period of time only because it is a distinct state of mind.

> This state of mind begins in Western Europe, but becomes worldwide. There begins to be a world civilization; and there can be no such thing without mental world-contemporane-

ity; we are all moderns together. The distinctive note of the epoch is human self-reliance, technically implemented. A human know-how is everywhere in demand; and therefore the underlying sciences universally claimed.

Human self-reliance naturally displaces reliance on God, so far as God is called on to meet human need. The word "Humanism" stands for the principle of displacement. The Modern World extends its human self-help by degrees; but it knows its method. We may look on the entire period as a progressive experiment in getting on without God in all-important practical matters.

Modernity begins with this method, at first a method of thought and then a method of tools. Its principle is very simple; purposes and wishes play no part in Nature; mathematics tells the full and exact story; causes are equal to effects, and therefore are alike in kind. The equation is the perfect language for describing what happens; and also the perfect instrument for prediction and techniques. The playroom for divine operation closes: God's purposes are simply irrelevant.

The Modern World thus moves towards a practical atheism, not by intention, but by default. Nietzsche's startling "God is dead!" is only a more violent statement of the mild words of Laplace: *"I have no need of that hypothesis."* A superfluous hypothesis becomes quietly and rightly a discarded hypothesis. In a world in which human beings are willing and able to do the hard thinking essential to scientific mastery, God has nothing in particular to do.

We must, I believe, be wholly in accord with this loyalty of the Modern World to the scientific method which has been the source of its power. We have only two notes of criticism: the "religion" it denounces is not religion; the "God" it gets along without is not God.

Certainly, a person like Albert Schweitzer, who brings to

Lambarene the full equipment of scientific medicine, has not found the meaning of his religion or his God impoverished by his science. Nor did Mahatma Gandhi find his own sense of God impaired by his work at Sabarmati, using modern veterinary methods in his hospital for ailing cattle.

What I wish to make clear is this: that the wide modern drift toward an implicit atheism—toward a naturalism which negates supernature, a secularism which coddles the human wish, a Laique conception of the good life and of politics—that drift is based upon a valid denial of a false idea of God.

For whatever God means, God is not a substitute for, nor a competitor with, the sciences and arts of modernity.

God is not an object among objects; nor a power among powers; nor a cause among causes; nor a medicine among medicines.

But if God is none of these things, what is God?

I say that the only genuine atheist is the person who holds that there are gulfs between right people and wrong people over which no bridge can be thrown. For God is that underlying unity of Being which is the permanent possibility of bridgemaking, for the Modern World as for all others, and without any sacrifice of its triumphs.

The Modern World has only to learn that, since there are no closed sciences, there are no economic solutions on economic grounds alone, no military solutions on military grounds alone, and what is harder, no legal solutions on legal grounds alone. Nor are conflict and competition to be abolished; but to be held within an all-human solidarity, in which the 'million masks of God' find dignity, respect, reverence.

# Alfred North Whitehead

William Ernest Hocking was a member of the Department of Philosophy at Harvard which invited Alfred North Whitehead, the British mathematician and philosopher of natural sciences, to come to these shores in 1924. He received word that he was being asked to teach not mathematics—which had been the subject he had taught for 40 years—but philosophy, the field of his concentrated thought expressed in such of his books as *The Philosophy of Physical Nature*. To his wife, Whitehead exclaimed, "There is nothing in the world that I would rather do." When they arrived in the Harvard Square community in 1924, an astonishing transformation took place with respect to his productivity. He delivered a series of Lowell Lectures on *Science and the Modern World* in 1925. Following this classic work, he delivered in the very next year Lowell Lectures on *Religion in the Making*. This little book abounds with aphoristic wisdom and insight, containing phrases such as the movement from God the Void, to God the Enemy, to God the Companion. The following year saw the publication of *Symbolism: Its Meaning and Effect*. Only two years later, in 1929, his magnum opus arrived: *Process and Reality: An Essay in Cosmology*. In the very same year, two other volumes by him were published: *The Function of Reason* is one; the other is a gathering of essays on *The Aims of Education*. Other works followed.

Born in 1861, Alfred was the son of an Anglican clergyman who was head of a private school. He was educated in the classical mode: ancient languages, classical authors, mathematics and the Bible, which was read in Greek. In addition to his formal courses at Trinity College, University of Cambridge, his higher education was vigorously advanced by membership in an undergraduate group called The Apostles, which engaged in incessant conversation on matters pertaining to the whole of cultural life. Started by Tennyson in 1820, The Apostles met at 10 on Saturday evening and continued to anytime Sunday morning.

Whitehead's marriage to Evelyn Willoughby added immensely to his aesthetic sensitivity; she taught him that beauty is the aim of existence. A biography of Bertrand Russell describes Russell's enduring but unrequited love for Evelyn Whitehead. The Whiteheads had three children, one of whom was shot down during World War I. Their daughter long was a familiar sight in Harvard Square. The other son taught at the Harvard Business School, and Mrs. T. North Whitehead, his wife, is a person with whom I worked as a member and officer of the Cambridge Historical Society.

Alfred North Whitehead's thought, as seen in his published writings, falls into three main periods. Mathematics and logic engaged his primary attention from the end of the nineteenth century to World War I. He wrote *A Treatise on Universal Algebra*, then the monumental *Principia Mathematica* with Russell—"a landmark in the study of logic"—as well as a popular University Library *Introduction to Mathematics*.

From 1917 until he left for Harvard, Whitehead's focus was the philosophy of physical nature. He wrote *The Organization of Thought: Educational and Scientific, An Enquiry Concerning the Principles of Natural Knowledge, The Concept of Nature*, and *The Principle of Relativity*.

His third period, the Harvard years, dealt with cosmology, metaphysics and civilization. What Whitehead's thought has contributed to civilization may be surmised by the concluding sentence of Charles Hartshorne's interpretation of Whitehead's metaphysics:

"The basic principles of our knowledge and experience, physical, biological, sociological, aesthetic, religious, are in this philosophy given an intellectual integration such as only a thousand years or ten thousand years of further reflection and inquiry seem likely to exhaust or adequately evaluate, but whose wide relevance and, in many respects, at least comparative accuracy some of us think can already be discerned."

As you contemplate the wisdom offered to us by Alfred North Whitehead, listen to a few of his bold words concerning God:

> God is the ideal companion, the mirror which discloses to every creature its own greatness.

> God is not to be treated as an exception to all metaphysical principles, invoked to save their collapse. God is their chief exemplification.

> God is the beginning and the end.

> God is dipolar.

> It is as true to say that God is one and the World many, as that the World is one and God many.

It is as true to say that God creates the World, as that the World creates God.

God is the great companion—the fellow-sufferer who understands.

We find here the final application of the doctrine of objective immortality. Our immediate actions perish and yet live for evermore.

God is in the world, or nowhere, creating continually in us and around us. This creative principle is everywhere, in animate and so-called inanimate matter, in the ether, water, earth, human hearts.

Creation is a continuing process. Insofar as we partake of this creative process we partake of the divine, of God, and that participation is our immortality. Our true destiny as cocreator in the universe is our dignity and grandeur.

# Charles Hartshorne

Charles Hartshorne is our fifth person to be celebrated as a philosophical interpreter of a new world view which includes a new view of God. His relation to the other four Harvard Square philosophers—Peirce, James, Hocking, and Whitehead—is both pervasive and important.

Hartshorne was born north of Pittsburgh in 1897 in Kittanning, Pennsylvania, where his father was an Episcopal clergyman. He received his A.B. from Harvard College in 1921, his M.A. in 1922 and his Ph.D. in philosophy in 1923. He says it was his first teacher in philosophical theology, William Ernest Hocking, who introduced him to the idea of a God not in every sense absolute, and yet in the religious sense perfect. When he returned to Harvard in 1925 after postgraduate study in Europe, he was a research assistant in the Department of Philosophy and was asked if he would edit the papers of Charles Sanders Peirce, which were in the department's possession. Then knowing little of Peirce, he later invited a fellow philosopher, Paul Weiss, to join him in the vast task. Together they edited the definitive initial six volume *Collected Papers* published by Harvard University Press.

Hartshorne's admiration for William James includes not only the psychologist and philosopher's impact on world thought but his literary genius, and the fact that he was a great man and not just a great intellect. As for Whitehead, Hartshorne is a primary living interpreter of the Anglo-American philosopher's thought. While working on the Peirce papers, he was Whitehead's teaching assistant and frequently visited the home of Professor and Mrs. Whitehead. In 1946, when Charles Hartshorne was teaching philosophy at the University of Chicago (and when I was in the College there), I had the good fortune to buy his early classic, *Man's Vision of God and the Logic of Theism*. Then, during my years of graduate work, I not only chose to take various courses with him—including courses of individually directed research—but also became more personally related through The First Unitarian Church of Chicago where he and his wife, Dorothy, were church members. Inasmuch as I was the church's Director of Student Work, I sometimes invited him to speak at our weekly Channing Club meetings or to be one of the speakers at our series of William Ellery Channing Lectures presented on campus at the University, which was

49

just across the street from the Church.

On the basis of what I first learned in these years, I discovered that Charles Hartshorne is the Einstein of religious thought. For three quarters of a century, his primary attention was given to the idea which includes all ideas—the idea of God. He has applied severe canons of logic to the idea of God in the great systems of thought old and new, East and West. He has placed before us the exact and exhaustive alternatives between which we may—and indeed must—choose. His own conclusion is that the all-inclusive actual-potential Whole is literally the ever-living and eternal God. Listen for yourself, then, to these words of Charles Hartshorne:

> Secular knowledge supports the religious idea of God if, and only if, by religion is meant something quite distinct from what has passed as orthodox theology.

> My conviction is that a magnificent intellectual content— far surpassing that of such systems as Thomism and positivism—is implicit in the religious faith most briefly expressed in three words: God is love.

> Under present world conditions it may seem peculiarly difficult to conceive of divine love. but divinity is not the privilege of escaping all sufferings but the exact contrary of sharing them all. Faith in love is not belief in a special kind of magic. Social awareness is the essence of God and the human ideal.

> Love is desire for the good of others, ideally all others. Being ethical does not mean never injuring anyone; for the interests of others may require such injury. Being ethical means acting from love; but love means realization in oneself of the desires and experiences of others, so that one who loves can inflict suffering only by undergoing suffering oneself, willingly and fully.

> Love involves sensitivity to the joys and sorrows of others. The ultimate motive is love, which has two equally fundamental aspects, self-love and love for others. Neither is ever in human affairs totally unmixed with the other.

God is not the being whose life is sheer joy and beauty, but the cosmic sufferer.

The cosmos is held together by love. Cosmic being is cosmic experience, is cosmic sociality or love. Love is the highest wisdom and the most far-reaching power.

All meaning implicitly asserts God, because all meaning is nothing less than a reference to one or other of the two aspects of the cosmic reality, what it has done or what it could do—that is, to the consequent or primordial natures of God.

The world as preserving its identity through all transformations is infinitely endowed with power to assimilate variety into unity. Indeed, the world in this sense is identical with God. God is the self-identical individuality of the world somewhat as a person is the self-identical individuality of his or her ever-changing system of atoms.

Does this not introduce tragedy into God? Yes, existence is tragic for God. It is tragic for any being that loves those involved in tragedy. And this is why we can literally love God, because we are parts of God's internal life.

God is the socially differentiated whole of all things which only love of all things can explain. We are parts of God, God as a unity in variety.

# CONCLUSION

How shall we assess the contribution to human thought made by these five philosophers whose discovery has been described as America's new vision of God? That term is used in order to stress the convergence of a new worldview shared by these thinkers' evolving system of ideas. Although we are too close in time and space to be able to speak with truly reliable perspective, I suggest that it may not be inappropriate today to wonder if this both old and new vision of reality may not bear comparison with events which occurred in the axial age which gave birth to great civilizations of the Earth in both the East and the West.

## Recommended Reading

*Philosophers Speak of God* by Charles Hartshorne and William L. Reese (Amherst, N.Y., 2000).

*The Rise of American Philosophy: Cambridge, Massachusetts 1860-1930* by Bruce Kuklick (New Haven: Yale University, 1977).

*Founders of Constructive Postmodern Philosophy: Peirce, James, Bergson, Whitehead and Hartshorne* by David Ray Griffin and others (Albany: State University Press of New York, 1993).

# PART III

## God and The Modern World

# Preface

"God and the Modern World" is a theme which has been a precious part of my liberal ministry since 1960.

In addition to hosting occasional annual events at the continental General Assembly of the Unitarian Universalist Association, I have done the same on a small scale for many years with respect to colloquium gatherings at Harvard University, where I served as one of the chaplains. Our invited speakers for these informal colloquia open to the public were natural scientists, social scientists, and humanities faculty and practioners. These events were presented by the Cambridge Forum, of which I was the director for twenty years.

# The Struggle for Power and Peace

## William Ernest Hocking

*In 1960 the first* Colloquium on God and the Modern World *occurred at the May Meetings of the American Unitarian Association. The speaker in the Harvard Square Meetinghouse of the First Parish in Cambridge, Unitarian, was William Ernest Hocking, Alford Professor,* Emeritus, *of Natural Religion and Moral Philosophy, Harvard University. Dr. Hocking spoke on "God and the Modern World—With Special Reference to the Present World Struggle for Power and Peace."*

The "Modern World" is a distinct period of time only because it is a distinct state of mind.

This state of mind begins in Western Europe, but becomes worldwide. There begins to be a world civilization; and there can be no such thing without mental world-contemporaneity; we are all moderns together. The distinctive note of the epoch is human self-reliance, technically implemented. A human know-how is everywhere in demand; and therefore the underlying sciences universally claimed.

Human self-reliance naturally displaces reliance on God, so far as God is called on to meet human need. The word "Humanism" stands for the principle of this displacement. The Modern World extends its human self-help by degrees; but it knows its method. We may look on the entire period as a progressive experiment in getting on without

God, in all-important practical matters.

Modernity begins with this method, at first a method of thought and then a method of tools. Its principle is very simple; purposes and wishes play no part in Nature; mathematics tells the full and exact story; causes are equal to effects, and therefore alike in kind. The equation is the perfect language for describing what happens; and also the perfect instrument for prediction and technique. The playroom for divine operation closes: God's purposes are simply irrelevant.

The Modern World thus moves toward a practical atheism, not by intention, but by default. Nietzsche's startling "God is dead" is only a more violent statement of the mild words of Laplace, "I have no need of that hypothesis." A superfluous hypothesis becomes quietly and rightly a discarded hypothesis. In a world in which men are willing and able to do the hard thinking and observing essential to scientific mastery, God has nothing in particular to do. This applies first of all to the physical sciences: it extends to all the rest, the sciences of life and of man. Each of these, taking physics as an ideal, tends to become a "closed science," admitting considerations only of kinds pertinent to its specific problems, excluding the irrelevant. We develop a pure biology, excluding any irrelevant notions of design; a pure economics of wealth and welfare (Adam Smith, Ricardo), a pure science of Law (John Austin and followers), a pure political science of power (Hobbes to von Treitschke). Even in the sciences of man and society, God becomes the permanently irrelevant consideration.

Looking over its more than three centuries of increasingly confident pursuit, this experiment of getting on without God is endorsed by world-changing success. Discovery, invention, human mastery surpassing everything hitherto known. Not that everything has succeeded, but that we know we are on the right track: we are at home with Nature; we know how to tackle residual problems; we know where to look for remedies and where not to look. True, we have run into a period of the gravest disorder and possible catastrophe that mankind has ever faced. But nothing in these troubles discounts the scientific method, or the axiom of Relevance. On the contrary, the appalling threat is a witness to our achievement in the analysis and control of nuclear energies. We cannot repudiate these powers merely because we have not tamed them. There is no going back on Science or Technology.

There is indeed a serious question whether the closed physical sciences are a sufficient model for the closed sciences of life, subhuman and human. Allowing that God's purposes are irrelevant, must there not be some local or indwelling purposes in the phenomena of life of all stages? And if we allow goal-seeking as a factor in the description of organisms singly, must we not be prepared to admit a total drive, an elan vital, in the evolution of all life, which intimates a divine guidance? Such questions intrude themselves.

The scientist must share the universal human impulse to sympathize with the processes of nature, to participate first emotionally and then morally in the rhythm of the seasons, the growth, the reproduction, the beauty of living things. If Kepler could not keep out of his speculations on the planetary orbits his prejudice that the ellipse is more beautiful than the circle, and therefore more appropriate for God's design of the heavenly harmony, we may expect what actually happened—recurrent protest against pure mathematical objectivity, continued reassertion of the inveterate animism of man's fellowship with Nature, a refusal to be alienated by the purge of purpose from inner participation in the total cosmic process. The resistance all along the line from Diderot and the Romantics, from Goethe and Lamarck to Whitehead's great campaign against the "bifurcation of Nature" must not be overlooked.

But the Humanist cause remains valid for the principle of self help. And for that reason, the "Scientific Revolution"—as Sir Charles Snow has called it (Rede Lecture, Cambridge)—becomes a social and moral cause. Those who persist in calling on God to cure disease, regulate the weather, prosper the crops, determine the outcome of childbirth, dispel poverty, are held traitorous to the cause of enlightened responsibility. The Modern World becomes a foe of all religion that invokes God to do what man should and can do for himself. To call such religion "opiate of the people" (wrongly ascribed to Marx) might fairly describe the spirit of the entire Modern World, Marxian and non-Marxian, in its campaign for objectivity.

# I
# Truth and Fallacy in the Modern Trend to Atheism

We must, I believe, be wholly in accord with this loyalty of the Modern World to the scientific method which has been the source of its power. We have only two notes of criticism:

the "religion" it denounces is not religion;

the "God" it gets along without is not God.

Certainly, a man like Albert Schweitzer, who brings to Lambarene the full equipment of scientific medicine, has not found the meaning of his religion or his God impoverished by his science. Nor did Mahatma Gandhi find his own sense of God impaired by his work at Sabarmati, using modern veterinary methods in his hospital for ailing cattle.

What I wish to make clear is this: that the wide modern drift toward an implicit atheism—toward a naturalism which negates supernature, a secularism which coddles the human wish, a Laique conception of the good life and of politics—that drift is based upon a valid denial of a false idea of God.

For whatever God means, he is not a substitute for, nor a competitor with, the sciences and arts of modernity.

God is not an object among objects; nor a power among powers; nor a cause among causes; nor a medicine among medicines.

But if God is none of these things, what is God?

Are we to fall back on mystery; or on Spinoza's dictum that all determination is negation—nothing specific can be said; or on the Mahayana Void; or on the Tao, unnameable and nonassertive?

Or shall we look closer into ourselves, with the insight which Mohammed of old shares with the Existentialist of today: "God is nearer to you than the great vein in your neck"?

Both of these proposals have substance. The mystics are right in refusing to identify God with any tangible object. And driven to use imagery, the believer is in constant peril of literalizing the metaphor—polytheism does just that. A scrupulous faith is accordingly driven to reticence; and it may reach the point of declining to specify what it is it believes in: one "has Faith"—enough said! I once thought this an irresponsible evasion; I now think better of it. It makes an important distinction between the man capable of purpose and the drifter. Judgment of a shrewd employer.

Faith, period, is a way of "accepting the universe." Santayana's picture of "animal faith" is not inappropriate to the human situation: there is an elan of all living things, including man, toward an environment assumed auspicious. We are, as Existentialists inclined to say, "engaged" in a context of being, postulated as offering the possibility of a rewarding life-career. The spontaneous attitude of the human infant, including his protests, is essentially that of Faith, period.

Nevertheless, the thinking animal must bring to his self-steering enterprise something better than a blank chart. While every concept applied to God is open to criticism—"God is power, will, creativity" (Whitehead disallows all of these)—our Modern World, indisposed to mysticism, finds it incredible that anything absolutely important can be absolutely indefinable.

Let us turn to the second proposal, that we look more closely into ourselves—toward the central region of selfhood—toward what I incline to call the kernel or nucleus of experience. For it is through intimate experience that we have direct traffic with "Reality"—and "God" must be a name for the most Real.

This inner being of ours, this moving current of feelings, sensations, imaginations, incipient purposes, is aware of itself as among other selves, all occupied with objects but not identical with them.

The self knows that *it* is not an "object": it cannot be severed from its subjectivity, its feelings and purposes, and remain itself. It knows also that the other selves are not measurable objects, calculable and predictable and manageable, as if devoid of purpose. It knows that this life of will is more real than the being of "objects" thus controllable.

Hence, to say that God is not an object among objects is to imply—not that God lacks something of reality—but that objects lack something. Our objects are contents of experience which we can treat as purposeless for a purpose, the purpose of control, reserving ourselves and all selves from the objective field. We see in part why God cannot be an object.

But God may be—and I suggest he is—present to us as a demand, among other things a demand to think. We find ourselves summoned to reject a passive existence of immersion in sensation, and to live in a world of things, events, laws, common to all selves. We are stirred to take our private experience as universal, so that it may enter the fabric we call Truth, valid for all.

That summons to objective living, to come out of subjectivity and enter a context in which language, engagements, laws become possible—in which science itself becomes possible—is not that the call of Reality? Let us test this suggestion by the experience of such a user of science as Mahatma Gandhi, asking him what he means by the term "God." By good fortune, we have his words:[1]

> There is an indefinable mysterious power that pervades everything. I feel it, though I do not see it.... It defies all proof because it is so unlike all that I perceive through my senses....
>
> I do feel that there is orderliness in the universe. There is an unalterable law governing everything and every being that exists and lives. It is no blind law; for no blind law can govern the conduct of living beings.... That law which governs all life is God: *Law and the Lawgiver are one...*
>
> I do dimly perceive that while everything around me is ever changing, ever dying, there is underlying all that changes a living power that is changeless,
>
> that *holds all together,*
>
> that creates, dissolves, and re-creates.
>
> That informing power or spirit is God...
>
> But he is no God who merely satisfies the intellect, if he ever does:
>
> God, to be God, *must rule the heart and transform it...*
>
> He who would, in his own person, test the fact of God's presence can do so by a living faith . . . [by a resolve] to believe in the moral government of the world, and therefore in the supremacy of the moral law, the law of Truth and Love . . . [together with] a clear determination summarily to reject all that is contrary to Truth and Love. [The fruit, a "realization more real than the five senses can ever produce,

proved by the transformed conduct and character of those who have felt the real presence of God within."]

I confess I have no argument to convince through reason: Faith transcends reason....

All that I can advise is not to attempt the impossible.

Gandhi's words are words of experience addressed to experiencers. He speaks of a *law which can be "felt"*—a law of order in world process which is also a moral law: but to be aware of this law is to feel it as a call to duty,—hence his remarkable sentence, "Law and the Lawgiver are one." To put this in our own terms, let us say that human experience is inseparable from a sense of direction, having a certain authority, as if to say, "This way lies your road to fulfillment." (It is perhaps the human form of that biological endseeking which Bergson calls *élan vital.*) Our experience is anything but a stream of factual data which we passively receive. There are active elements of address to us, a stir from without—calling for response from within. (The old Confucians were definitely on the right track in speaking of *Ming,* a decree of Heaven, an appointment or task.) Since we are all seekers for direction, and for our own meaning, no one can be unaware of this touch of summons, in which the listener, whether or not he uses the word God, finds the added dimensions of Companionship, of Duty, of Destiny.

If this is the case, it is only through the awareness of the Direction-giver that human life becomes fully human, as lived in the presence of a higher court of judgment and care. Through this awareness, solitariness is relieved both of its sting and of its indifference—the barbaric freedom of Fling. Religion is "the redemption of solitude." There can be no genuine Humanism without God.

With this understanding, some features of our Modern World come to clearer light.

## II

## The Modern World Not Satisfied with Itself

If I am right in holding that the trend to a secular civilization in our Modern World is essentially a justified rejection of a false idea of God and of religion, but without filling the empty place, we should expect some indications of discomfort. We find them.

We find in recent studies of this period much use of the term "revolution" to indicate, not violent political changes, but radical shiftings of power within society due to persistent pressures of new insights and techniques, leaving much unfinished business. In this sense our entire Modern period may fairly be considered revolutionary. This, I judge, is part of what Sir Charles Snow has in mind, as "The Scientific Revolution," of which we have spoken. He finds it leading to an ominous division between the culture based on science and the traditional culture based on the wider human interests. But as it happens, another historian calls attention to a malaise of conscience within this field, working its way toward definite remedy, by way of a later and more specialized revolution.

Mr. Adolf Berle is concerned with a single phase of recent economic development. He speaks of the corporation, which in the guise of a fictitious person has had a long legal history, with specified rights and duties defined in charters issued by existing public powers. Technically subject to these powers, the corporation through its actual synthesis of services—social and moral as well as economic—has become a power quasi-political in character and extent, and thereby a danger with which various law-systems have tried to cope by way of limitation and division. But the new power maintains itself, under the most various constitutions, as Berle convincingly shows, in part by a revolutionary development of its own conscience —whence his title *The 20th Century Capitalist Revolution.*[2] The "soulless" corporation begins to develop a soul, and to adopt the total culture of the community as a responsibility, beyond the requirements of existing law, and beyond its own technical interests. As Berle states the matter, corporations assume that "somehow there is a *higher law* which imposes itself in time on princes and powers and institutions of this terrestrial earth"—somewhat in the spirit of Augustine's "City of God." They thus move toward closing the gap, justly noted and feared by Sir Charles Snow, which their own power, if used with a Frankenstein cynicism, must render disastrous.

I pass no judgment on this estimate of contemporary corporate tendencies. I can verify some of them. I merely point out that this "higher law" discerned by Berle is never out of operation: it cannot be escaped, because it belongs to the consciences of individuals who make up every social grouping.[3] And once our attention is directed to its working, we can observe its action on a much wider area than that of the corporation.

For just because Modernity undertakes to apply the methods of science to all social concerns, it is obliged to become clear as to what human welfare consists in, to assume the right to work for it and to make any changes in institutions necessary to achieve it. In no field does this attitude make more difference than in the science of law. Law can be viewed as an expression of eternal justice, or as the will of a sovereign more or less disposed to justice; in these lights it has a certain stability. But if we consider law a means for reaching social ends, it invites mankind to tamper with their own institutions, to accept nothing merely as inherited or as sacred; to make them over freely nearer to the heart's desire. It is just this to which the Modern World arrived, stirred by Bentham and Mill, and especially by a studious German, von Ihering, whose book on *The Purpose in Law (Der Zweck im Recht, 1877)* formulated the spirit of the times. This spirit duly gave birth to the sociology of law—a revolution in attitude fundamental to all revolutions, and conceivably making violent revolutions unnecessary.

But if law becomes a means to an end, a guide to what Dean Pound calls "social engineering," we must know what we want society to be. And it becomes increasingly evident that just this social ideal cannot be read from the surface of our daily wishes, whether in field or factory, in home or school, in mass communication or in foreign policy—everywhere there are considerations we call moral which prevent us from setting up a legal program based solely on a calculus of wishes. The "higher law" begins to appear as a necessity for guidance, even in the literalities of economics and in the practical work of law-making.

This is true of the domestic problems of economic origin—labor and management—employment, taxation, social security. It is doubly true of international issues, which almost always have an economic core. (In 1938, Herbert Feis, economic adviser in the State Department, after enquiries in East Europe, remarked to me "Since the turn of the century, economics has not been a closed science; there are no economic solutions with ethical solutions.") Foreign policy must consider national interest; but in the world of today, a world of nations, national interest is not enough. There are no political solutions, without solutions in the higher court. The closed-science ideal of Modernity breaks down completely: *THERE ARE NO CLOSED SCIENCES.*

## III
## The Conditions of World Unity

The fact that we live in a world of nations implies a possible clash of national interests, even apart from the explicit enmity imbedded in the Soviet ideology. Every foreign policy must aim at peace, since war is now intolerable. But no foreign policy can seek peace by appeasement, which means yielding principle to threat, and abandoning not only national interest but national character. If there is to be a moral factor in statecraft, there must be an absolute; God is the absolute. This set of demands appears to be a prescription for rigidity and rigidity may be a synonym for death.

The defect in this picture is that it omits a factor of will-changing, through achieved identity of purpose. The central defect of national purposes hitherto is that they have stopped at the local interest: they have failed to see that each nation must take for its province the world. This implies coalescence of domain, at the periphery: an impossible conception unless people can agree on the general characteristics of the political world. It is precisely here that the role of God appears, if we re-gard God as the moral unity of the world, the summons to an identical good. If there is a moral absolute, it is a ground on which people must necessarily agree, when once they grasp its meaning. The only hopeful statecraft for today is one which employs the power of this necessity. It is likely to involve what I have called a "creative risk," an act which assumes the necessary identity, and thereby brings it into actual effect.

And whoever uses this necessary identity to bring about agreement of will, I should regard as a man of Faith, no matter what his profession. Let me illustrate by an example present to all our minds. The lamented Albert Camus is commonly classed as an atheist: he denies the God he considers—rightly or wrongly—the God of the Church. He equally denies Nihilism and drift. And since he thus denies absolute denial, he is implicitly asserting an affirmative faith. What is it he believes in?

In his great book, *The Rebel,* he struggles through the long history of revolt against injustice, and against conventional beliefs, arriving at a clear contrast between rebellion and revolution. Revolution—as vio-lent overturn—exchanges one tyranny for another, he finds. Rebellion has a different temper—it unites denunciation of tyranny with a call for agreement. It stands up to the tyrant—only not to destroy him, but to bring him to himself. He says to him, in effect: "This which you require of me is *against your own nature* as well as mine. At the peril of my life I refuse to do it, in the name of our common humanity." What the Rebel achieves—if he does achieve it—is solidarity instead of conflict. He has created a new mind in the tyrant, by an act of affirmative faith.

His risk is real; but it is based on a certitude. He knows his perception of right to be no private sentiment, but a necessity for all men, hence commanding the tyrant as well, if he will fairly face himself. That certitude is of the nature of a religious faith.

Camus does not state his principle in these words. Nor does he say that he has here introduced a new and important principle into modern ethics and politics. I take the responsibility of saying this for him. He describes the principle of the Rebel's action as follows: "It is the refusal to be treated as an object.... It is the affirmation of a nature common to all men, which eludes the world of power.... [It implies] 'I rebel, therefore we exist'."[4] This type of statecraft is impossible for two sorts of men: those who insist on perfect security, where there is no security; and those who have resigned all inner certitude, in view of what they regard as the insight of the Modern World—the universal relativity of all convictions. If this were the last word of the Modern World, I should feel it incompetent to win either peace or power. But it is not the last word for the placing of relativity within the framework of truth—one of the present preoccupations both of modern physics and modern logic.

Camus's power for peace may be the greater because he does not address himself directly to the statesmen, but to the artists. He knows that the task has to do with the "collective passions" of our time, and that it is the nature of art to stir multitudes at once. He hopes that a courageous art may "end by revealing the 'we are,' and with it, the way to a burning humility,"[5] conscious of working with an invincible power in history.

I refer again to Albert Schweitzer, for whom the spell of music is one way of his own assertion of solidarity across gulfs—as it was also for Van Cliburn. The appeal of the universal in human dignity and the equally eternal appeal of the universal in beauty are both integral parts of the work of God in the world.

But the necessary certitude cannot be prescribed as a diplomatic resource. If the statesman or the artist is without it, nothing could be more disastrous than to pretend it. It is true that there is an inescapable bond of union between man and man, whatever the differences, but in every individual impasse, the route of union must be sought and felt, as one in darkness prays for light. The sought-for light, when it comes, appears as a resolution of contradictions and conflict, perhaps rather in the tempers of approach than in the detail of the issues; there comes a certitude of union in the will-to-solve, wherein the actual solution ceases to be impossible.

It is for this reason that I say that the only genuine atheist is the man who holds that there are gulfs between right man and wrong men over which no bridge can be thrown. For God is that underlying unity of Being which is the permanent possibility of bridgemaking, for the Modern World as for all others, and without any sacrifice of its triumphs.

The Modern World has only to learn that, since there are no closed sciences, there are no economic solutions on economic grounds alone, no military solutions on military grounds alone, and what is harder, no legal solutions on legal grounds alone.

For law assumes the settled identity of the subjects of law, whereas in the international field it is precisely the identity of the national entities that is in constant flux and conflict, not to be solved by abolishing the nation. Nor are conflict and competition to be abolished; but to be held within an all-human solidarity, in which the "million masks of God" find dignity, respect, reverence.

# Endnotes

1    "Mahatma Gandhi, His Spiritual Message." Columbia Masterworks. Record 17523-D.

2    Berle, Adolf A. Jr., *The 20th Century Revolution* (N. Y.: Harcourt, Brace, 1954).

3    Hocking, William Ernest, "Though our Capacity for a Double Morality Impedes Its Way to Dominance." *Strength of Men and Nations* (N. Y.: Harper, 1959), Ch. V.

4    Camus, Albert, *The Rebel* (N. Y.: Knopf, 1954: Vintage edition), p. 250.

5    *Ibid*, 275.

# A Modern View of God

**Charles Hartshorne**

*The second Colloquium* on God and the Modern World *was delivered in 1961 at the First Church in Boston in connection with the Annual Meetings of the American Unitarian Association. One of Dr. Hartshorne's notable books is* Philosophers Speak of God.

Why is the idea of religion without God so widespread today?

One reason, without a doubt, is the boost which technology has given man's self-esteem. Instead of turning to a superhuman power to influence nature in his favor he can turn to the engineer. Man apparently needs no outside help, he can help himself. Then there is the power of the human mind shown in pure science. Instead of thinking with awe how mysterious life is, we think how, step by step, the hidden causes of all that happens to us are being unraveled. Not only can man do almost all things, but more and more seems that he can know almost all things. He is himself potentially something like what God was believed to be actually. So man begins to worship his own kind. This self-deification of man is a chief rival in our time of what I regard as true religion. For I agree with the old Greeks, who agreed with the Hebrews at this point, that one of man's greatest enemies is his own vanity, *hubris*.

There are, however, several excuses for our modern falling deeply into hubris. Not only are our technology and pure science wonderful achievements, truly deserving to be glorified, but also these new powers encourage habits of thinking which in some respects make it more difficult to see grounds for belief in the superhuman. Science is our great theoretical accomplishment; yet it seems to uncover no evidence of anything divine. We have learned, or think we have learned, that what science cannot discover is very likely not there. If fairies and demons and witches were real, science would have had to invoke them to explain events. But it has no occasion to do so. Hence we cease to take such ideas seriously. The idea of God seems to many to belong in the same class, and we feel a certain obligation to be on the side of science, against fairy tales and nightmares.

Now I wish to argue that while all these reactions to the modern scene are natural enough, some of them do not withstand careful criticism and represent, indeed, aspects of a sort of fairy tale of science, not a tested scientific hypothesis.

So far as influencing nature is concerned, we have certainly immensely increased our resources. But the chief results of this change are: 1) the total number of people on earth has multiplied many times over, and has even become one of our gravest anxieties, a threat which only fatuous optimists belittle, 2) newborn babies have several times as good a chance of reaching maturity as they used to have, 3) those who reach maturity can expect to live a decade or two longer than formerly, 4) a minority of people on earth have luxuries undreamed of in older days even for kings, and 5) when things go wrong, there is usually something we can do besides pray—we can look for an expert, medical or other, and we have better reason to trust our modern experts than the primitive had to trust elders and medicine men. However, do these differences amount to anything, relative to the problem of God? I say that, relative to that problem, they are negligible. Each of us is still born and dies; each is still throughout life subject to accidental death or grievous injury and are still but a negligibly small part of a stupendous whole, which for all we know infinitely precedes and will infinitely outlast us. Though armed with atomic power, humanity is yet almost nothing in physical power compared even to the sun, and there are billions and billions of suns! On this earth now, we are powerful, but what are we in the vastness of reality? So close to nothing we can scarcely say how small, or how weak.

In what I have just said, I have employed facts of astronomy. I think, indeed, that the *proper* result of science is to increase human humility, to make our inveterate conceit seem even more absurd, if possible, than the Greeks and ancient Hebrews could know it to be. Think of millions of galaxies, each probably with millions of planets. Even though we do reach a few of these planets in space ships, the ones we do not reach will be practically the same in number as all those which exist. Thus the races of rational beings which, according to all reasonable probability, people the great spaces, will be virtually unknown to us forever. The Greeks could explore but a small portion of this earth; they estimated the total universe as a billion miles in diameter. We talk in billions of light-years. True, we can explore our solar system, and eventually perhaps a bit beyond, but our solar system dwarfs the area of the earth which the Greeks could reach no more than our present estimate of the universe dwarfs that of the Greeks. Understating the case, no larger part of the universe, relatively speaking, seems to astronomers today open to human exploration than ancient astronomers supposed was open to them. Our relative insignificance, therefore, according to our knowledge, has not diminished. Only human vanity has enabled us to imagine otherwise—to talk, for example, of conquering space.

I am not, please note, belittling science. It is one of our noblest, most glorious accomplishments. But one of the chief origins of science—Einstein has said it—is deep humility. We are the only terrestrial animal, though surely not the only animal, who can see ourselves as but an item in the scheme of things, not the center about which all must or can be made to turn.

There is another consideration. Ancient people might dream of existing forever on earth. They did not know that the sun's fires are temporary and must eventually burn out. We do know. We also know that the sun might become unbearably hot, and destroy us in that way. We know that we have but a temporary dwelling on this earth. Of course, some of us may colonize other planets and even solar systems. But still, every such venture will be risky, many will fail; success can never be guaranteed, and certainly there is no guarantee that the successful colonists will be such as we would be able to consider in significant degree our own descendants, or even that our influence will have been helpful to them. Add to this the fact, which we know far better than ancient people, that human folly could bring human life to an end at almost any time—in the near or distant future.

We are God and are infinitely far from being so. Rather we are tiny, and for all practical purposes ultimately temporary, as well as unreliable and often very cruel, creatures. Now there are two possibilities and only two: this tiny, temporary episode of nature called humanity either exists merely for its own sake, or also for the sake of something greater than humanity. If we in our own eyes exist merely for ourselves, then so far as our valuations go, the rest of the universe exists for us. We must either serve, or be served by, the larger cosmos. We cannot but use the cosmos, so far as accessible to us, just as the cells in our bodies cannot but profit by our organic existence enclosing them, but the cells in our bodies also serve us whether or not they have any feeling of doing so. One way to put the religious question is simply: "Do we in turn stand in an analogous relation to anything greater than ourselves in space time, and can we have any awareness of this relation?"

This question has no proper analogy to that of fairies. Fairies at most were incidental conveniences, or nuisances. But the question, "Is the part for the whole, or the whole for the part?" is not an incidental question. It is the question, if we set aside our natural self-centeredness and look at life objectively, as the astronomer does. Are we to live and die merely for humanity, and are the species of rational animals on other planets to live and die merely for themselves? Or do they, and all creatures, live and die for the whole encompassing them, as our cells do for us?

Science as I view it could not possibly favor the self-centered answer to this question. Science is not anthropomorphic. It does not assume any peculiar importance of human beings. The famous "rejection of final clauses" was really, in one aspect, a rejection of human favoring causes. Nothing cosmic turns, for science, upon human values in particular. Does it follow that nothing turns upon values of any kind? I believe this is a non sequitur. The ends of nature could only be incomparably vaster than merely human ends and, therefore, we in our amazing vanity cannot easily conceive these ends. But they can be conceived, as we shall see.

Still, you may say, it remains true that science finds no evidence of anything divine, and where there is no scientific evidence, have we not learned to admit that there is no evidence at all? Here it is pertinent to inquire what it means to speak of scientific evidence. The highest, or at least, a very high authority on the scientific method, in my opinion is Karl Popper. His view is that a hypothesis is scientific if it can be observationally falsified, not, please note, if it can be verified. For it is doubtful if, strictly speaking, any scientific generalization has been verified, that is, shown to be exactly true as it stands. So-called crucial experiments are not those which have a chance of proving some theory since no experiment can wholly establish a positive theory; but rather, those which have a chance of disproving a theory. One instance clearly not in accordance with a supposed law refutes the law, but many instances in conformity with the law still do not prove it. Accepting this test of falsifiability, we may remark that the idea of God either could, or could not, be falsified by some conceivable observation. If it could not, then theism is a view which science is in no position to test; and the fact that science has not "verified" theism is irrelevant. For as, Popper persuasively argues, to confirm a view by scientific evidence is only to conceive a way of falsifying it, and then to find that the falsifying observation fails to result from the suitable experimental or observational conditions. Who, then, has told us what an observation incompatible with theism would be like? Is it the observation that there are evils? In that case, science is not needed to evaluate theism, for this fact has always been known. And theists have always denied that the existence of evils contradicted their belief. If they are right in this, then how could science find evidence against the divine existence? Is any fact, other than evil, incompatible with that existence? Is it the reign of law in nature? But theists say that the laws of nature express the divine power and consistency.

What are we to conclude from the apparent fact that theism, as theists understand it, is not scientifically testable at all? We might conclude that theism has no consistent meaning, and hence could not be true. Or we might conclude that it has some meaning, but of a sort whose truth is untestable by human means. Finally, we might conclude that it has meaning, and that science is not the only human means of testing truth. This last is my position. I hold that the relevant test of ideas of God is their ability to integrate, not facts of science, but the principles which all science and all life presuppose, principles without which we could not understand how there could be facts at all, or why it is worth knowing what the facts are. Not facts, but the ideas of fact, not values but the idea of value, not truths but the idea of truth, is what theism tries to elucidate. The study which investigates such questions is philosophy. To suppose that natural science can substitute for philosophy in this task is logical confusion; it is pseudo science, not science.

Are theists right, however, in holding that the facts of evil and of the orderliness of nature are consistent with theism? I hold that they are right. However, I do not think that the classical, or best known, theologians and theistic philosophers have given us a very clear and consistent account of this matter, and I cannot blame anyone who concludes that they have failed to make their case. I shall now try to show how the case can be made.

It is useless to maintain that all evil is divinely designed and is but good in disguise, for on that principle all human choice is absurd. Do as you please, the result is exactly what divine wisdom saw to be needed for the perfection of the world plan. True, it may be a part of the plan that you should be punished for what you do, but still your deed is quite as it should be, for if it were not, it would not have been included in the providential design, and would not have happened. On this view, serving God means doing whatever you happen to do. You cannot go wrong. In addition to this absurdity, is the difficulty of distinguishing between such a God and the sadist who finds evil to his or her liking. God deliberately designs the evils, for they are necessary to the world's being pleasing to God.

It is also useless to explain evil as the result of human freedom alone, for all animate nature involves conflict and presumably suffering. Surely human choice throws no light upon this fact.

The root of the trouble is in failing to note the starting point for the problem of evil. This starting point is the notion that God creates. What is it to create? It is to determine the otherwise indeterminate. Out of the vagueness or chaos of the merely possible, comes the definiteness of the actual. There might be all sorts of worlds: yet this world came into being. Similarly, the poet might write all sorts of poems, but actually writes this poem, or this set of poems. Now suppose the divine poet includes in a poem a description of a lesser non-divine or human poet creating non-divine poetry. The divine poet can choose the description of this other and lesser poet and poetry just as is pleasing, can God not? No, this will not do, for the divine poet creates not just poems, but poets who create poems; and since to create is to decide how the vagueness of possibility is to pass into definite actuality, if the created poets really exist as poets, as creators, then they, and not the divine poet must decide in some degree what the non-divine poems are to be. I wonder if you see already how, according to this analysis, the problem of evil results from an equivocation of terms. According to the view which gives rise to the problem, God is to decide precisely what lesser agents decide; but then there can be no lesser agents, and all decisions are divine decisions. The supreme artist would thus create not lesser artists, but mere descriptions of artists, mere dreams of lesser creators. The one agent is, on that view, the only agent, but imagines others. We are these divine imaginings of lesser agents. But in that case, we could from our own experience have no concept of creation, of agency, of decision, with which to ascribe the supreme form of these powers to deity. The whole business is a play with ambiguities, and I believe it is nothing more.

Once you admit that the supreme artist must create lesser artists, with genuine, though inferior capacities for deciding what no one else has wholly decided for them, you will see that the perfection of divine power cannot consist of a monopoly of creative freedom. However well and powerfully God may decide, God must leave something for the creatures to decide. Hence it cannot be right to attribute the details of the world to divine decree, and it need not be wrong to attribute the evils of these details to decisions other than divine. Nor is it merely human creatures who must in some measure have creative power, for what could the supreme creative agent produce but lesser forms of creativity? There is no absolute difference between human originality and that of a humble animal tracing the design of its own individual life in fine details unique and never to be repeated. The jump from infinite creativity to the creature, even the humble creature, can hardly be from the infinite to zero; it must rather be from the infinite to the finite, from supreme creative freedom to lesser creative freedom, not no freedom. Any creature is thus somewhere between the total absence of discretionary power, and its eminent or divine form. In this way creaturely freedom explains not only evils which man produces but those which animals and atoms produce. The entire world, on a consistently theistic view, is pervaded by an element of self-determination in each and every individual whatsoever. Myriads of agents other than God have had a hand in any result, and it is therefore illegitimate to ask why God made that result as it is. God did not "make" it, if that means decide it, for the creatures are all, in part, self-decided.

Does it follow that we must renounce the perfection of the divine power? Not if words are used carefully. The perfection of the divine power does not consist of the ability to make merely unilateral decisions, for this is meaningless. Every agent and every creator produces results beyond itself only by influencing the self-determination of other agents, or other creators. Decision is always *shared*, so far as effects upon others are concerned. The perfect form of this shared decision means, not ideal ability to decide detailed results, but ideal ability to decide general outlines. These outlines are the laws of nature. Who but God could have decided these? They set the limits within which the lesser agents can effectively work out the details of their existence. Without such limits the universal creativity would mean universal chaos and frustration. With these limits, elements of chaos and frustration remain but they are subordinate to general order and harmony.

The orderliness of nature is essential to creaturely freedom. It can then, without inconsistency, be considered providential. That some evils result is not the fault of the order, for any order must stop short of destroying freedom, and freedom means risk.

To put the matter another way, the atheistic argument from evil holds that God must be weak or wicked in not using divine freedom to maximize harmony and reduce discord to zero. This means nothing if not this, that the chances of harmony and those of discord could and should be made to vary *inversely*. But we can, rather clearly, understand that this is logically impossible. Harmony and discord, as values, have the very same source, freedom. Harmony in freedom is good, conflict in freedom is evil, and the greater the freedom the greater the chances of both good and of evil. God is held deficient for not doing what logically could not be done. To avoid the evil of suffering and discord, God should have a world of pure puppets, incapable of getting off their designated tracks; to avoid the evil of deadly monotony and insipidity, to make existence interesting by causing free agents able to make their own decisions to flourish, he should not have a world of puppets at all, but self-determining creatures with some faint spark at least of creativity analogous to his own supreme creativity.

I see nothing in the classic "problem of evil" but this confusion or equivocation between creatures both puppets and free, or both lesser forms and not even lesser forms of the power of decision eminently ascribed to their creator.

The ideal power and wisdom of God does not, then, imply a perfection of detailed results, for no power could guarantee the detailed actions of others but rather an optimal excess of opportunity over risk, as arising from the laws of nature.

I cannot give anything like all my reasons for accepting this conception, but I wish to return to our previous question: "Is the part for the sake of whole, or the whole merely for the sake of the part?" To me it seems wonderfully irrational to suppose that the enduring universe exists merely for its transient parts, but if the parts exist for the whole, then the whole must contain the values of the parts. Since it is unintelligible that values can exist except for some being able to value or enjoy them, the cosmos should be thought of as able to value all that falls within it. The supreme creator is then the whole, evolving and appreciating its own parts, somewhat as the human body evolves new molecules, and in many cases new cells, from time to time; but the supreme whole must have full appreciation, such as we cannot have, for the details of the parts. The idea of the cosmos as conscious and evolving its own details, subject to their proper freedom is, I believe, compatible with all the results of science. True, there are many puzzles which may arise in this connection, but it is striking how few among the skeptics see that this is the question to which theists, if they understand themselves, give an affirmative answer. Most theists are unclear about this also, and many will say that I am quite on the wrong track, but I believe I have read these people with more care than they have read me, or anyone who thinks as I do.

I said above that science excludes not all final causes, but human favoring or anthropocentric final causes. I shall now try to explain this. One must first understand, once and for all, that no teleology can exclude unfortunate accidents and frustrations, for goals have to be reached through multiple acts of freedom, none of which can be entirely controlled, even by God. The point is not that God cannot control them, but that they cannot be controlled. It is not God's influence which has limits, but their capacity to receive influence. Absolute control of a free being, and there can be no others, is self-contradictory. Hence exceptional monstrosities and incidental sufferings are to be attributed to the chance results of freedom, not to the teleology of nature. Only the general plan, the structure of laws, the normal pattern of nature can be wholly purposive.

If you ask, must not the laws and the antecedent conditions entirely determine the detailed phenomena, the answer is, not if law is conceived as physicists now incline to conceive it, as essentially statistical, a matter of averages in a large group of similar cases. The new outlook in physics thus fits our doctrine of pervasive freedom, as the Newtonian outlook did not.

Granting then that details are not necessarily purposive, what are the goals which nature is realizing? Here older discussions, both theistic and antitheistic, suffered from arbitrary assumption. For instance, it was thought strange that all living creatures are subject to death, that species die out, that creatures live by destroying other creatures. I find all of these things less strange than the more or less unconscious beliefs which made them appear strange. Is it desirable for an individual to live forever? If the individual has no long run memory and foresight, it cannot matter to it that it will not live forever, and if the individual does not have long range memory and foresight, then in the long run continuation within the limits of its individuality will prove increasingly monotonous, lacking in interest and zest. All young animals show more evidence of being thrilled by life, the novelty of things, than old animals. Human beings are not exceptions, in principle. They only think they are. One has but to observe life to see this. So I conclude, endless continuation of the individual is either of no value to the individual, or it is undesirable, even unendurable. That species do not last forever is even more obviously not an evil. Species other than us cannot know that they are temporary, and we can understand how our temporary existence can contribute to what is not temporary, the all-encompassing Whole.

You may suppose that even the Whole, according to the same principle of diminishing novelty, must finally grow old and tired, but the whole is the supreme reality, with no external conditions limiting it; whatever novelty it may need, it should have full power to evolve. Only ideal power, divine power, can either sustain, or make desirable, endless continuation. So I think we can, quite consistently, conceive God as immortal, without giving up the argument that mortality for creatures is an evil for them. Something in reality must be permanent, and God, I submit, is precisely that something.

But should creatures live, while they do live, by destroying others? Is this not vicious or cruel? This too I deny. Granted that creatures should not live forever, how then are they to die? The only causes must be other creatures, either within, as parts, or without as members of the external environment. What harm does it do a deer that it dies through the attack of a lion, rather than of old age? Old age is a dull mode of existence; if death generally came that way, then instead of the species being composed mostly of creatures enjoying the prime of Life, it would be more largely composed of half bored elders. The sum of intense enjoyment would be less, not more.

What, we now ask, are the overall goals of nature? We have argued that the parts live not merely for their own sakes but for that of the whole. What does the whole get from the parts? Well, what do we get from our parts, our bodily cells and molecules? We get the sensory and emotional content of our experience. When our cells thrive, we feel physical pleasure; when they are injured, we often feel physical pain. Thus their health contributes to our joy, and their ill health to our sorrow. We seem to participate in their weal and woe in whatever sense they are subject to weal and woe. Cells are living—I believe sentient—individuals. The "love of God" has often been spoken of, but we may overlook the full meaning of our own words. To love is, at least, to participate in the life of another. It may be more than that, but we should not use the word for less. We love, then, our own cells, though without distinct consciousness, so far as the single cells are concerned. We have a vague sense of good and evil enjoyed by the parts of the body. Imagine this vague sense flooded with the light of full consciousness and you have an analogy for the love of God.

It is a well-known law that the value of experience as coming to us from the body depends upon the variety and intensity of activities which can be harmonized. We know that lack of variety and contrast kills interest; we also know that variety and contrast may in some cases confuse and disturb. Harmonious variety is essential to value. What is nature if not a wondrously varied pattern of forms. Is it an harmonious pattern? Not in the sense of excluding all conflict, discord, or suffering; but this we have seen to be inherent in the pervasiveness of freedom, without which there could be no world at all. Essentially nature is harmonious, things fit together in an ecological web which naturalists admire the more they study it. The laws of nature articulate the harmony of nature. Some of the greatest scientists have tried to tell us how their more or less mystical reverence for and enjoyment of the cosmic harmony inspires their work, but we have often been too dull to believe them. I take them at their word.

Nature is a harmony in variety, ultimately for the enjoyment of the whole, but proximately for the enjoyment of each and every part, in proportion to its awareness of this harmony. Variety is in space as well as in time. That individuals and species die and others take their place is variety in time. Those who lament the passing of species want to limit the variety to be enjoyed by the whole. Truly they know not what they would have.

Can God love us if we are allowed to cease while God lives on? The answer lies in a simple ambiguity in the word "cease." That our lives are finite in time as well as in space does not mean that at death we become nothing, or a mere corpse, for our past experiences are not canceled out. The past is indestructible, ever-living. Persons who truly love those who have died feel this vividly, though they usually, thanks to the strange blinders worn by philosophers and theologians who have taught them no better, misconceive the nature of the feeling. The past reality of the person is not dead and cannot die. It "lives forevermore," in Whitehead's phrase. Where? How? In the Whole, whose appreciation is infinitely tenacious of every item it once has appropriated. God forgets us never, and this is our immortality. We are imperishable items in God's consciousness.

Our vanity is perhaps not satisfied by this. I can only speak for myself. I wish no further immortality, either for myself or for those I love. It is this earthly life which should be dear to us, for which we should be grateful, and this life is deathless, for what we and those we have influenced have done and felt cannot ever not have been done and felt, but the ultimate summing up and treasuring of this imperishable reality is not in our memory of consciousness; it is in God's.

There will be those who say that the view I have been presenting is pantheistic, implying that this is enough to condemn it. The term "pantheism" has been used to cover doctrines as far apart from each other as from views commonly called theistic, and the habit of trying to put an end to reasonable discussion by the use of this label is on a par intellectually with terming every economic policy with which we disagree "communist." The communism which properly deserves rejection in principle is something much more definite that those who misuse the term have in mind; so with the pantheism which deserves rejection in principle. Or, in other words, if my view is pantheistic, then perhaps so much the better for (one form of) pantheism, not necessarily so much the worse for my view.

The foregoing conception of God, or something like it, can be found, apart from my own writings, in Fechner's *Zend Avesta*, written a century ago, in Berdyaev's *Destiny of Man*, and in the last chapter of Whitehead's *Process and Reality*. Many other writers have pointed in its direction. It is the great neglected alternative to classical theism, the stone rejected by the builders, whose ultimate destiny has by no means been decided by this rejection.

But how, you may ask, can we know any such view to be true? The answer to this question is a long story, but it can summarized in brief as follows: that philosophy is true which contains in itself the explanatory power of its rival, plus additional power of its own. The theory of pervasive freedom explains evil at least as well as any other view could do, for freedom is always risk, but the theory explains good better than the other view, provided we admit a supreme or divine level of freedom, by whose influence all lesser freedom can be benignly guided and coordinated, for freedom thus coordinated is primarily opportunity, and only secondarily risk. Thus freedom, if taken as both divine and non-divine is self-explanatory, accounting alike for its failures and its successes. It is the only self-explanatory principle. Order is due to the overruling supremacy of divine freedom, disorder to the multiplicity of lesser freedoms.

An interesting, but complicated, matter to reconsider is the historical proofs for the existence of God in the light of this modern doctrine. I find that in spite of the attacks of Hume, Kant, and others, they can all be restated so as to have a certain cogency.

These attacks rest upon assumptions incompatible with the theory of pervasive freedom, and of divine freedom as that of the all-inclusive reality. If we are not to be victimized by mistakes of our ancestors, the entire problem of God must be viewed afresh. I deeply believe that the idea of a God who determines all things is an absurdity; and I also deeply believe that religion without God is a poor second best, an irrational self-deification of humanity in our dangerous pride. Our life is on earth, not elsewhere; but the eventual importance of earthly life consists of its contribution to the cosmic Life, which alone is truly immortal, and alone deserves to be worshipped.

# God at the End of the Century

**John E. Smith**

*The 1989 General Assembly of the Unitarian Universalist Association was held at Yale University. The speaker at the Colloquium* on God and the Modern World *was John E. Smith, Clark Professor of Philosophy at Yale and a primary interpreter of American philosophy and philosophy of religion.*

In his opening address for this Colloquium series in 1960, William Ernest Hocking took note of the growth of self-reliance in the modern world and what he called a "progressive experiment in getting on without God." He added, however, that the "God" the modern world proposes to get along without is not God in the most legitimate sense and hence that the entire situation calls for reinterpretation. I believe that Hocking was right in his judgment, and we must now attempt to consider the bearing of what has happened in the intervening decades to the notion of God.

To begin with, the underlying problem determining the odyssey of belief or disbelief in God over the past century involves a tension between the Theistic conception of God as omniscient, omnipotent, unchanging and fully complete, on the one hand, and the reality of time, history, human freedom and creativity, on the other. This tension manifests itself along two parallel lines: first, the belief that arose

82

in the Renaissance and finally reached a radical conclusion in our time, that the traditional idea of God is totally incompatible with human initiative, choice and action for which we are responsible. This line of thought holds that God is an obstacle to human self-realization and that humans can be, exist and act, only if God is *not*. The second line of thought points to terrifying problems that have arisen under the aegis of the belief that human beings can create themselves out of their own freedom; this belief warns against the consequences of the slogan that "God is dead, all is permitted." There is truth and error in both of these responses, and I propose to explore each of them briefly as a prelude to suggesting how it may be possible first, to reconcile an intelligible idea of God with the reality of time, history and human freedom; secondly, to deal with the exaggeration of freedom which has led to a new rejection of God and the creation of a secular void.

Let us begin with the problems that have arisen in the modern world, as the result of retaining the traditional God of Theism endowed with the now familiar attributes of omnipotence, omniscience, completeness and utter transcendence. Behind the use of these attributes was the belief that they are expressions of the superlatives necessary for giving God the highest praise and honor. Accordingly, it was inconceivable that God should have less than total power, knowledge, perfection and transcendence. And so it might appear, were it not for two fundamental ideas contained in the Western religious tradition which run counter to this conception. The two ideas are: first, that there is a real historical order, which includes novelty, growth, creativity and human initiative; secondly, the belief that God is living and participates in the direction of this historical order. The problem is, how can we reconcile these two ideas with the God of the traditional attributes each of which implies that God cannot take history seriously and, being already complete, cannot be related to a world of change including the novelties presented by human action?

A brief look a history will help to make these ideas clearer. While I do not agree with those who claim that the ancient religious thinkers went wrong when they adopted the principles and concepts of Greek philosophy for framing the doctrine of God, I do believe that the critics are right at one point. In the general drift of Greek thought there was a definite bias in favor of the fixed and the static over the dynamic and changing. This feature found its way into the Western tradition of thinking about God and thus created the major problem. What is to become of the reality of history, of human freedom, change and development if God is static perfection? Is the unfolding of history a kind of cosmic appearance, a mere show in time that is without ultimate significance in the divine economy? Can we conceive of God in such a way as to understand how the novelty and creativity we find in the historical order can make a difference to God?

These and similar questions have no answer if God is understood solely in terms of static perfection, already so complete and self-contained that the novelties of history simply vanish into an eternity that has no relation to time. It is a great irony that the Western religious tradition, unique in its recognition of time and history, should have held on so long to a conception of God which has no place for either. This irony, moreover, is not the result of speculations by philosophers but is inherent in the religious tradition itself. If the historical order and the individuals acting in it are both real, it is totally incoherent to think of God in such a way that they lose that reality and are excluded from the divine knowledge and understanding. The God who knows all, can do everything and in whom all aims are already realized, does not make sense not only as a matter of rationality but of religious coherence as well. While the tradition believed in a living God whose presence is felt in history, the God of Theism does not allow for either.

William James wrestled with this problem many decades ago when he opposed Josiah Royce's early philosophy of the Absolute or the God in whom all error and evil are already overcome. What is the significance, he asked, of our striving as moral beings to do what is right, to overcome evil and injustice in the world, if in God the triumph is already assured and the evil fully nullified. To James that belief not only leaves us with no tasks to perform or, as he put it, allows us "moral holidays," but robs our most heroic moral efforts of all significance in the eyes of God as well. According to James, God "gives you indeed the assurance that all is well with Him and his eternal way of thinking; but thereupon he leaves you to be finitely saved by your own temporal devices." Kierkegaard made much the same point when he declared that Hegel's God absconds to the realm of pure Being leaving the rest of us to face the worst!

The key to resolving the problem is to be found in an idea that is not new but which until recently has been forgotten. It is the idea that the power of God is not the same as its indiscriminate use, but rather that God treats creatures in accordance with their own natures. The power exercised over stars and stones is one thing; the power exercised over human beings is quite another. On this view, there is room for finite agents and our limited, but real, capacity for freedom even if, as has so often happened, that freedom turns out to be destructive.

The conflict between the reality of our striving and the belief that all goals are already realized in the Divine life can be overcome only if we can free ourselves of the idea that, while we experience time in the familiar order of past, present and future, God sees everything at once in an Eternal Now. That idea was no doubt meant to be a way of praising God by distancing divine from human knowing, but a little reflection shows that this is not so. God, on any intelligible interpretation, cannot know *less* than we do and what we do know must be included in the divine knowledge. But if this is so and we experience time as a serial order that involves a real future, then it cannot be true to say that God knows nothing of this temporal order but only of an Eternal Present into which the future vanishes. The solving idea here is that the events that may happen tomorrow are in one most important feature also future for God. Let us say that God continues to sustain the general structure of the world—things in space, events in time, causes and effects and indeed all the continuities that we rely upon in the cosmic order. There is, however, one element in the future which is not already "there" even for God; that is the decision and action of the individual seeking to realize him or her self in a process of development. Such decisions and actions come into being only in their time, and before that they were possibilities not yet made actual. Accordingly, through these possibilities there is left to us a measure of freedom in the world. In any case, it does no honor to God to conceive divine knowledge as an all-at-once affair so that God could not know the temporal order *as temporal* but only as eternal; hence God would fail to know something that we as finite creatures know. That is a curious consequence indeed.

The problem of reconciling the being of God and the reality of human freedom has had a special significance on the American scene because of Americans' heightened awareness of the individual and our abundant energy. One of the chief reasons why the monarchical and sometimes even tyrannical God of the older Puritan tradition lost ground in the succeeding centuries was the sense that such a God—being the sole source of power—reduces human beings to the level of mere things. But as we have seen and as Charles Hartshorne has pointed out in many writings, there is no need to conceive of God in this monolithic way, especially when in doing so we go against the belief in a God of time and history, which has been so powerful in the Western tradition. The eclipse of the God before whom we lose our status as free and responsible agents, would be salutary and would, moreover, clear the way for the recovery of a more coherent faith.

I turn now to the second of the two lines of thought concerning God and freedom which I noted at the outset. This idea also began with the Renaissance thinkers; their belief in the dignity of the human person was so enlarged upon in the succeeding centuries that it became in our time a doctrine of total self-creation. If, as we have seen, the Absolute God leaves us, in James' phrase, with nothing to do, the doctrine of radical freedom, as we *shall* see, leaves God with nothing to do.

The Renaissance philosophers were struck by a singular feature of human beings, namely that while the creatures of the natural world were thought to have be assigned a fixed place in the cosmic scheme, human beings alone were allotted no such place because, through freedom, their task was to determine their own place. The idea was that there is a sliding scale, so to speak, with the angels at one end and the beasts at the other; human beings have the power to determine their place within those limits. Along with this power went a mandate, a clear paraphrase of the Bible, to multiply and develop the resources of the earth. According to this view, human beings become the special agent of God in continuing the work of creation.

The belief in human freedom as self-determination was later given its most lasting expression by Immanuel Kant in his doctrine of autonomy; we are to be determined neither by what is above us nor by what is beneath, but only by self-legislating freedom. Kant just stopped short of the more radical doctrine of freedom which was to make its appearance in our time. For Kant, we inherit a natural endowment and while we do not have a fixed nature like stars and stones, neither do we create ourselves from nothing. Kant saw no conflict between this increasing autonomy and the being of God, but rather conceived of the moral law within us as, in his own words, the stern daughter of the voice of God. Kant, moreover, could speak of human beings as having freedom and being capable of forging a character that endures, but he did not go as far as later thinkers in declaring that, man **is** freedom through and through.

The final chapter in the odyssey of freedom in the modern world was to be written by Sartre and his Existentialism, but there was an intermediate step taken in the last half of the nineteenth century which forms an important part of the story. The growth of the Industrial Revolution in the countries of Europe led to mass societies made up of great numbers of workers and members of the lower middle class. Thinkers as far apart as Kierkegaard, Marx and Nietzsche gave voice to the growing concern that mass society meant anonymity, facelessness and the loss of individuality. In different ways and for disparate reasons these thinkers issued a summons, a call to individuals to become acutely aware of their own existence and to recover a sense of their responsibility to establish an integral self. For Kierkegaard, of course, the call to self-possession was intimately related to faith in God, whereas for Nietzsche especially and Marx to a lesser extent, the reality of God was seen as the major obstacle to human self-development and hence the call for the death of God.

The Existentialism of Jean-Paul Sartre carries this line of thinking to its ultimate conclusion. Since we are now to regard ourselves not merely as having freedom, but as being freedom, freedom can be realized only if God is not. Notice the radical feature of this idea: it is more than an atheism based on skepticism about any arguments for the existence of God; it is instead a desperate claim that the reality of God would mean disaster and the nullification of human freedom. This claim shows itself most clearly in Sartre's project, namely, that the task of man is to be his own creator; in short, to *be* God. In developing this theme, Sartre, ironically enough, chose the same monarchical conception of God which, as we have seen, led to the difficulties considered in the first part of our discussion. Fastening on the idea of God as *causa sui* or totally self-caused, Sartre declared that it is precisely the project of man to be his own cause or to create himself out of nothing. James and Hartshorne, you will recall, wanted to reinterpret the idea of God to resolve the problem of freedom; Sartre is more radical by rejecting God altogether and replacing the divine prerogative with the absolute freedom of human individuals. The question which did not seem to occur to Sartre is whether we may not have more to fear from an absolute freedom in human hands than that same freedom in the hands of God.

It is my contention that we are now and have been for some time experiencing the consequences of the dismissal of God and the exaggeration of a human freedom that knows no limits beyond itself. As I read the signs, the absence of strong convictions about the reality of God has served to create a secular void, a sense that human existence is purposeless, is devoid of value and no longer has any sacred significance. And indeed we may well ask whether anything is sacred in our time, unless it be the drive to succeed. It seems that we have forgotten an old but important truth: the need for a commitment to a Ground and Goal of life is a need that is as basic to our existence as the need for food and clothing. James never tired of insisting on this truth and underlined it in the subtitle he attached to *The Varieties of Religious Experience*—"A Study in Human Nature." If we do not find a basic orientation in life, an overarching purpose having authority over our conduct in a God of Love and Truth, we shall find ourselves falling into the hands of some idol—wealth, quest for power, esthetic enjoyment and especially our own dear selves—that manifests the demonic. No one of these limited and evanescent goals can, so to speak, bear the weight needed to sustain a meaningful life in so precarious a world as the one in which we live.

What I have called the secular void is a most dangerous vacuum, but it does not really remain empty since it will invariably be filled by something less than God. Recent events suggest that there have been two main responses by those who experience this void in their own lives and are alarmed by it. On the one hand, there is the worship of charismatic figures who promise deliverance from the emptiness and chaos of the contemporary scene; on the other hand, there is a yearning to revive an older form of religion that has not kept pace with the intellectual, social and cultural developments of the past few decades. Consider what has been happening on what we may call the popular religious front and how clearly these events give evidence of the two responses. We have witnessed the multiplication of religious cults, the hypnotic appeal of would-be saviors, and the frenzy of fanaticism, all of which represents desperate attempts to fill the void. The second response manifests itself in the resurgence of evangelical piety rooted in the belief that the efforts of religious thinkers in recent years to maintain a high standard of intelligence in religion and to relate religious faith to the problems of society represent just so much falling away from what is envisioned as authentic biblical religion. The phenomenon of the electronic church, taken in its full sweep, provides a vivid illustration of the attempt to fill the spiritual vacuum by going back to a conservative, and in many instances, a fundamentalist religion which long ago lost its hold on those who have a high regard for religious intelligence. I do not believe that either of these responses is adequate for dealing with the crisis of nihilism and meaninglessness which I have called the secular void.

The attraction of the charismatic individual and the mesmerizing power such a person commands springs chiefly from a promise of deliverance and a vision of a new order free from the corruptions of the current world. That promise would call forth no loyalty were it not for a strong sense, more often than not on the part of the young, that some sort of deliverance is needed. The tragic saga of Jonestown and the People's Temple in Guyana is the paradigm case. The Rev. Mr. Jones held out a promise of deliverance which, as became all too evident, he could not deliver. There is, of course, no litmus paper test of the sincerity and authenticity of any messianic person, but there are at least three fundamental criteria by which some rational judgment can be made. In the first instance, such a person becomes demonic if he or she claims to be the absolute object of devotion; secondly, no charismatic person should claim exemption from the ethic imposed on the followers; and thirdly, no money or property should be solicited which are not put to visible work for human welfare, but remain instead at the secret disposal of the leader. It is quite doubtful that the Rev. Mr. Jones passed any of these tests. Nor was he alone. More recently we have witnessed the dark shadow of numerous television ministries, and the specter of Elmer Gantry rises once again. Threatening as the secular void is, it cannot be overcome in this way.

The way of evangelical revival, or what is essentially the resurgence of Protestant conservatism in religious belief, presents no better solution and is in fact retrogressive. The reappearance of an anti-intellectualistic frame of mind with its opposition between "book-learning" and "having the spirit" falls into the error that Jonathan Edwards exposed two and a half centuries ago in his critical appraisal of the Great Awakening. "True religion," he declared, "cannot be all heat and no light." There is, moreover, a new anti-scientific spirit accompanying the new religious fervor; and it threatens to undo all that has been accomplished in this century in overcoming the senselessness of the so-called warfare between science and religion. If current views of Creation-science, for example, represent the biblical message, Moses would surely have been astounded, if indeed it would have made any sense to him at all. The return of the old claim of biblical inerrancy and of supposedly literal interpretations of the Bible sets at naught the devoted work of two or more generations of scholars bent on making the texts available and intelligible to the modern reader. These scholars were dedicated to the proposition that there is a God of truth and that no truth is God's enemy.

Finally, returning to the simple model of the two story universe with Nature below and Supernatural above and the picture of God as one being among others nullifies the contributions of Niebuhr, Tillich, Maritain, Herberg, Brightman, Bertocci and Hartshorne in their wrestling with theological and philosophical problems. Their concern to relate ancient religious wisdom to the growth of knowledge and to understand the relevance of new patterns of thought is rejected by religious conservatism. In short, much of the new religious concern now making itself felt is not likely to engage those who have become alienated from belief in God because the same disregard for intelligence motivates the new religious right.

Many people at present find themselves in something of the position of Job who was willing to accept all the calamities that plagued him if only he could gain some understanding of the nature of the God he trusted. Job could *withstand* his troubles, but he also wanted to *understand* God.

In closing, let me attempt a very brief summary. Reconciling the reality of God with human freedom requires reinterpretation and the overcoming of the monarchical conception of God which actually runs counter to the tradition itself. Reality is not one seamless whole, total and complete, but contains real possibilities which, in turn, mean a real future yet to come. In those possibilities, we, as beings who can decide and act, move and have our being. The idea of an absolute, human freedom that led to the dismissal of God is an exaggeration; we do not and cannot create ourselves out of nothing. The absence of God, moreover, creates a secular void that cannot be filled either by cults and charismatic figures or by a return to an outworn faith. The monstrous problems of the present—the growth of terrorism and the erosion of civilized life, the fearsome power of the drug culture, the two-edged sword of our technology and the violation of human rights by repressive regimes—all testify to what happens when freedom has no limits set from beyond ourselves. No religious solution, however, is possible as long as we retain a conception of God in which people cannot sincerely believe. But, as we have seen, there is no need to perpetuate that idea of God.

Hocking, in the end, was right: the "God" whose death has been widely proclaimed is not God.

# A Common Faith

**John Dewey**

*John Dewey stands as America's most notable twentieth-century public philosopher, reckoning with the practical problems of modern society as well as the perennial theoretical issues of philosophy. His classic* Terry Lectures *at Yale embody his distinctive reckoning with religion.*

Never before in history has mankind been so much of two minds, so divided into two camps, as it is today. Religions have traditionally been allied with ideas of the supernatural, and often have been based upon explicit beliefs about it. Today there are many who hold that nothing worthy of being called religious is possible apart from the supernatural. Those who hold this belief differ in many respects. They range from those who accept the dogmas and sacraments of the Greek and Roman Catholic Church as the only sure means of access to the supernatural to the theist or mild deist. Between them are the many Protestant denominations who think the Scriptures, aided by a pure conscience are adequate avenues to supernatural truth and power. But they agree on one point: the necessity for a Supernatural Being and for an immortality that is beyond the powers of nature.

The opposed group consists of those who think the advance of culture and science has completely discredited the supernatural and with it all religions that were allied with belief in it. But they go beyond this point. The extremists of this group believe that with the elimination of the supernatural not only must historic religions be dismissed but with them everything of a religious nature. When historical knowledge has discredited the claims made for the supernatural character of the persons said to have founded historic religions; when the supernatural inspiration attributed to literatures held sacred has been riddled, and when anthropological and psychological knowledge has disclosed the all-too-human source from which religious beliefs and practices have sprung, everything religious must, they say, also go.

There is one idea held in common by these two opposite groups: identification of the religious with the supernatural. The questions I shall raise concern the ground and the consequences of this identification: its reasons and its value. I develop another conception of the nature of the religious phase of experience, one that separates it from the supernatural and the things that have grown up about it.

Any activity pursued on behalf of an ideal end against obstacles and in spite of threats of personal loss because of conviction of its general and enduring value is religious in quality. The question narrows itself to this: Are the ideals that move us genuinely ideal or are they ideal only in contrast with our present state?

The import of the question extends far. It determines the meaning given to the word "God." On one score, the word can mean only a particular Being. On the other score, it denotes the unity of all ideal ends arousing us to desire and actions. Does the unification have a claim upon our attitude and conduct because it is already, apart from us, in realized existence, or because of its own inherent meaning and value? Suppose for the moment that the word "God" means the ideal ends that at a given time and place one acknowledges as having authority over his volition and emotion. The values to which one is supremely devoted, as far as these ends, through imagination, take on unity. If we make this supposition, the issue will stand out clearly in contrast with the doctrine of religions that "God" designates some kind of Being having prior and therefore non-ideal existence.

The idea that "God" represents a unification of ideal values that is essentially imaginative in origin when the imagination supervenes in conduct is attended with verbal difficulties owing to our frequent use of the word "imagination" to denote fantasy and doubtful reality. But the reality of ideal ends as ideals is vouched for by their undeniable power in action.

These considerations may be applied to the idea of God, or, to avoid misleading conceptions, to the idea of the divine. The idea is, as I have said, one of ideal possibilities unified through imaginative realization and projection. But this idea of God, or of the divine, is also connected with all the natural forces and conditions—including human associations—that promote the growth of the ideal and that further its realization. We are in the presence neither of ideals completely embodied in existence nor yet of ideals that are mere rootless ideals, fantasies, utopias. For there are forces in nature and society that generate and support the ideals. They are further unified by the action that gives them coherence and solidarity. It is this *active* relation between ideal and actual to which I would give the name "God." I would not insist that the name *must* be given.

A clear and intense conception of a union of ideal ends with actual conditions is capable of arousing steady emotion. It may be fed by every experience, no matter what its material. In a distracted age, the need for such an idea is urgent. It can unify interests and energies now dispersed; it can direct action and generate the heat of emotion and the light of intelligence. Whether one gives the name "God" to this union, operative in thought and action, is a matter for individual decision. But the *function* of such a working union of the ideal and the actual seems to me to be identical with the force that has in fact been attached to the conception of God in all religions that have a spiritual content; and a clear idea of that function seems to me urgently needed at the present time.

One reason why personally I think it fitting to use the word "God" to denote that uniting of the ideal and actual which has been spoken of, lies in the fact that aggressive atheism seems to me to have something in common with traditional supernaturalism. I do not mean merely that the former is mainly so negative that it fails to give positive direction to thought, though that fact is pertinent. What I have in mind especially is the exclusive preoccupation of both militant atheism and supernaturalism with humanity in isolation. For in spite of supernaturalism's reference to something beyond nature, it conceived of this earth as the moral center of the universe and of human beings as the apex of the whole scheme of things. It regards the drama of sin and redemption enacted within the isolated and lonely soul as the one thing of ultimate importance. Apart from humanity, nature is held either accursed or negligible. Militant atheism is also affected by lack of natural piety. The ties binding us to nature that poets have always celebrated are passed over lightly. The attitude taken is often that of our living in an indifferent and hostile world and issuing blasts of defiance. A religious attitude, however, needs the sense of our connection, in the way of both dependence and support, with the enveloping world that the imagination feels is a universe. Use of the words "God" or "divine" to convey the union of actual and ideal may protect human beings from a sense of isolation and from consequent despair or defiance. A humanistic religion, if it excludes our relation to nature, is pale and thin, as it is presumptuous, when it takes humanity as an object of worship.

Were the naturalistic foundations and bearings of religion grasped, the religious element in life would emerge from the throes of the crisis in religion. Religion would then be found to have its natural place in every aspect of human experience that is concerned with an estimate of possibilities, with emotional stir by possibilities as yet unrealized, and with all action on behalf of their realization. All that is significant in human experience falls within this frame.

The things in civilization we most prize are not of ourselves. They exist by grace of the doings and sufferings of the continuous human community in which we are a link. Ours is the responsibility of conserving, transmitting, rectifying and expanding the heritage of values we received that those who come after us may receive it more solid and secure, more widely accessible and more generously shared than we have received it. Here are all the elements for a religious faith that shall not be confined to sect, class, or race. Such a faith has always been implicit the common faith of humanity. It remains to make it explicit and militant.

—From *A Common Faith* by John Dewey (New Haven: Yale University Press, 1934).

# God and the World

**Alfred North Whitehead**

*During his years of teaching philosophy at Harvard University, Alfred North Whitehead aroused newly intense questions concerning God and the World. Here are some selections from* Religion in the Making, Science and the Modern World, *and* Process and Reality.

## I
## Religion and Science

During many generations there has been a gradual decay of religious influence in European civilization. Each revival touches a lower peak than its predecessor, and each period of slackness a lower depth. The average curve marks a steady fall in religious tone. In some countries the interest in religion is higher than in others. But in those countries where the interest is relatively high, it still falls as the generations pass. Religion is tending to degenerate into a decent formula wherewith to embellish a comfortable life. A great historic movement on this scale results from the convergence of many causes. I wish to suggest two of them.

In the first place, for over two centuries religion has been on the defensive, and on a weak defensive. The period has been one of unprecedented intellectual progress. In this way a series of novel situations have been produced for thought. Each such occasion has found the religious thinkers unprepared. Something, which has been proclaimed to be vital, has finally, after struggle, distress, and anathema, been modified and otherwise interpreted. The next generation of religious apologists then congratulated the religious world on the deeper insight which has been gained. The result of the continued repetition of this undignified retreat, during many generations, has at last almost entirely destroyed the intellectual authority of religious thinkers. Consider this contrast: when Darwin or Einstein proclaim theories which modify our ideas, it is a triumph for science. We do not go about saying that there is another defeat for science, because its old ideas have been abandoned. We know that another step of scientific insight has been gained. Religion will not regain its old power until it can face change in the same spirit as does science.

My second reason for the modern fading of interest involves the ultimate question of what we mean by religion. Religion is the reaction of human nature to its search for God. The presentation of God as an all-powerful arbitrary tyrant behind the unknown forces of nature awakens every modern instinct of critical reaction. This is fatal; for religion collapses unless its main positions command immediacy of assent. The psychology of modern civilizations is largely due to science, and is one of the chief ways in which the advance of science has weakened the hold of the old religious forms of expression. The non-religious motive which has entered into modern religious thought is the desire for a comfortable organization of modern society. Religion has been presented as valuable for the ordering of life. Its claims have been rested upon its function as a sanction to right conduct. Also, the purpose of right conduct quickly degenerates into the formation of pleasing social relations. We have here a subtle degradation of religious ideas, following upon their gradual purification under the influence of keener ethical intuitions. Conduct is a by-product of religion—an inevitable by-product, but not the main point. Every great religious teacher has revolted against the presentation of religion as a mere sanction of rules of conduct.

Religion is the vision of something which stands beyond, behind, and within, the passing flux of immediate things; something which is real, and yet waiting to be realized; something which is a remote possibility, and yet the greatest of present facts; something that gives meaning to all that passes, and yet eludes apprehension; something whose possession is the final good, and yet is beyond all reach; something which is the ultimate ideal, and the hopeless quest.

The fact of the religious vision, and its history of persistent expansion, is our one ground for optimism. Apart from it, human life is a flash of occasional enjoyments lighting up a mass of pain and misery, a bagatelle of transient experience. The vision claims nothing but worship, worship with the motive force of mutual love. The vision never overrules. It is always there, and it has the power of love presenting the one purpose whose fulfillment is eternal harmony. Evil is the brute motive force of fragmentary purpose, disregarding the eternal vision. Evil is overruling, retarding, hurting. The power of God is the worship God inspires. That religion is strong which in its ritual and its modes of thought evokes an apprehension of the commanding vision. The worship of God is not a rule of safety—it is an adventure of the spirit, a flight after the unattainable. The death of religion comes with the repression of the high hope of adventure.

# II
# God

Today there is but one religious dogma in debate: What do you mean by "God"? And in this respect, today is like all its yesterdays. There are three main simple renderings of this concept before the world.

1. The Eastern Asiatic concept of an impersonal order to which the world conforms. This order is the self-ordering of the world; it is not the world obeying an imposed rule. The concept expresses the extreme doctrine of immanence.

2. The Semitic concept of a definite personal individual entity, whose existence is the one ultimate metaphysical fact, absolute and underivative, and who decreed and ordered the derivative existence which we call the actual world. This Semitic concept is the rationalization of the tribal gods of the earlier communal religions. It expressed the extreme doc-

trine of transcendence.

3.  The Pantheistic concept of an entity to be described in the terms of the Semitic concept, except that the actual world is a phase within the complete fact which is this ultimate individual entity. The actual world, conceived apart from God, is unreal. Its only reality is God's reality. The actual world has the reality of being a partial description of what God is. But in itself it is merely a certain mutuality of "Appearance," which is a phase of the being of God. This is the extreme doctrine of monism.

It will be noticed that the Eastern Asiatic concept and the Pantheistic concept invert each other. According to the former concept, when we speak of God we are saying something about the world; and according to the latter concept, when we speak of the world we are saying something about God.

The Semitic concept and the Eastern Asiatic concept are directly opposed to each other, and any mediation between them must lead to complexity of thought. It is evident that the Semitic concept can very easily pass over into the Pantheistic concept. In fact, the history of philosophical theology in various Mahometan countries—Persia, for instance—shows that this passage has often been effected.

The main difficulties which the Semitic concept has to struggle with are two in number. One of them is that it leaves God completely outside metaphysical rationalization. We know, according to it, that God is such a being as to design and create this universe, and there our knowledge stops. If we mean by God's goodness that God is the one self-existent, complete entity, then God is good. But such goodness must not be confused with the ordinary goodness of daily life. God is undeniably useful, because anything baffling can be ascribed to God's direct decree.

The second difficulty of the concept is to get itself proved. The only possible proof would appear to be the "ontological proof" devised by Anselm, and revived by Descartes. According to this proof, the mere concept of such an entity allows us to infer its existence. Most philosophers and theologians reject this proof: for example, it is explicitly rejected by Cardinal Mercier in his *Manual of Scholastic Philosophy.*

Any proof which commences with the consideration of the character of the actual world cannot rise above the actuality of this world. It can only discover all the factors disclosed in the world as experienced. In other words, it may discover an immanent God, but not a God wholly transcendent. The difficulty can be put in this way: by considering the world we can find all the factors required by the total metaphysical situation; but we cannot discover anything not included in this totality of actual fact, and yet explanatory of it.

Christianity has not adopted any one of these clear alternatives. It has been true to its genius for keeping its metaphysics subordinate to the religious facts to which it appeals.

In the first place, it inherited the simple Semitic concept. All its founders naturally expressed themselves in those terms, and were addressing themselves to an audience who could only understand religion thus expressed.

But even here important qualifications have to be made. Christ himself introduces them. How far they were then new, or how far he is utilizing antecedent thought, is immaterial. The point is the decisive emphasis the nations receive in his teaching. The first point is the association of God with the Kingdom of Heaven, coupled with the explanation that "The Kingdom of Heaven is within you." The second point is the concept of God under the metaphor of a Father. The implications of this latter notion are expanded with moving insistence in the two epistles of St. John, to whom we owe the phrase, "God is love."

Finally, in the Gospel of St. John, by the introduction of the doctrine of the Logos, a clear move is made towards the modification of the notion of the unequivocal personal unity of the Semitic God. Indeed, for most Christian Churches, the simple Semitic doctrine is now a heresy, both by reason of the modification of personal unity and also by the insistence on immanence. The notion of immanence must be distinguished from that of omniscience. The Semitic God is omniscient; but, in addition to that, the Christian God is a factor in the universe. A few years ago a papyrus was found in an Egyptian tomb which proved to be an early Christian compilation called "The Sayings of Christ." Its exact authenticity and its exact authority do not concern us. I am quoting it as evidence of the mentality of many Christians in Egypt during the first few Christian centuries. At that date Egypt supplied the theological leaders of Christian thought. We find in these Logia of Christ the saying, "Cleave the wood, and I am there." This is merely one example of an emphatic assertion of immanence, and shows a serious divergence from the Semitic concept.

Immanence is a well-known modern doctrine. The points to be noticed are that it is implicit in various parts of the New Testament, and was explicit in the first theological epoch of Christianity. Christian theology was then Platonic; it followed John rather than Paul.

# III
# The Quest of God

The modern world has lost God and is seeking God. The reason for the loss stretches far back in the history of Christianity. In respect to its doctrine of God, the Church gradually returned to the Semitic concept, with the addition of the threefold personality. It is a concept which is clear, terrifying, and unprovable. It was supported by an unquestioned religious tradition. It was also supported by the conservative instinct of society, and by a history and a metaphysic both constructed expressly for that purpose. Moreover, to dissent was death.

On the whole, the Gospel of love was turned into a Gospel of fear. The Christian world was composed of terrified populations.

"In flaming fire taking vengeance on them that know not God, and that obey not the gospel of our Lord Jesus Christ"; says Paul. "Who shall be punished with everlasting destruction from the presence of the Lord, and from the glory of his power." (II Thessalonians 1:8-9)

The populations did well to be terrified at such ambiguous good tidings, which lost no emphasis in the promulgation.

If the modern world is to find God, it must find God through love and not through fear, with the help of John and not of Paul. Such a conclusion is true and represents a commonplace of modern thought. But it is only a very superficial rendering of the facts.

As a rebound from dogmatic intolerance, the simplicity of religious truth has been a favorite axiom of liberalizing theologians. It is difficult to understand upon what evidence this notion is based. In the physical world as science advances, we discern a complexity of interrelations.

There is a certain simplicity of dominant ideas, but modern physics does not disclose a simple world.

To reduce religion to a few simple notions seems an arbitrary solution of the problem before us. It may be common sense; but is it true? In view of the horrors produced by bigotry, it is natural for sensitive thinkers to minimize religious dogmas. But such pragmatic reasons are dangerous guides.

This procedure ends by basing religion on those few ideas which in the circumstances of the time are most effective in producing pleasing emotions and agreeable conduct. If our trust is in the ultimate power of reason as a discipline for the discernment of truth, we have no right to impose such a priori conditions. All undue simplifications of religious dogma are shipwrecked upon the rock of the problem of evil.

As a particular application, we may believe that the various doctrines about God have not suffered chiefly from their complexity. They have represented extremes of simplicity, so far as they have been formulated for the great rationalistic religions. The three extremes of simple notions should not represent in our eyes mutually exclusive concepts, from among which are to choose one and reject the others.

It cannot be true that contradictory notions can apply to the same fact. Thus reconcilement of these contrary concepts must be sought in a more searching analysis of the meaning of the terms in which they are phrased.

# IV
# God and the World

The notion of God as the "unmoved mover" is derived from Aristotle, at least so far as Western thought is concerned. The notion of God as "eminently real" is a favorite doctrine of Christian theology. The combination of the two into the doctrine of an aboriginal, eminently real, transcendent creator, at whose fiat the world came into being, and whose imposed will it obeys, is the fallacy which has infused tragedy into the histories of Christianity and of Mahometanism. When the Eastern world accepted Christianity, Caesar conquered; and the received text of Western theology was edited by his lawyers. The code of Justinian and the theology of Justinian are two volumes expressing one movement of the human spirit. The brief Galilean vision of humility flickered throughout the ages, uncertainly. In the official formulation of the religion, it has assumed the trivial form of the mere attribution to the Jews that they cherished a misconception about their Messiah. But the deeper idolatry of the fashioning of God in the image of the Egyptian, Persian, and Roman imperial rulers, was retained. The Church gave unto God the attributes which belonged exclusively to Caesar.

In the great formative period of theistic philosophy, which ended with the rise of Mahometanism, after a continuance coeval with civilization, three strains of thought emerge which, amid many variations in detail, respectively fashion God in the image of an imperial ruler, God in the image of a personification of moral energy, God in the image of an ultimate philosophical principle. Hume's *Dialogues* criticize unanswerably these modes of explaining the system of the world.

The three schools of thought can be associated respectively with the divine Caesars, the Hebrew prophets, and Aristotle. But Aristotle was antedated by Indian and Buddhist thought; the Hebrew prophets can be paralleled in traces of earlier thought; Mahometanism and the divine Caesars merely represent the most natural obvious, theistic idolatrous symbolism, at all epochs and places.

The history of theistic philosophy exhibits various stages of combination of these three diverse ways of entertaining the problem. There is, however, in the Galilean origin of Christianity yet another suggestion which does not fit very well with any of the three main strands of thought. It does not emphasize the rule of Caesar, or the ruthless moralist, or the unmoved mover. It dwells upon the tender elements in the world, which slowly and in quietness operate by love.

Apart from any reference to existing religions as they are, or as they ought to be, we must investigate dispassionately what the metaphysical principles here developed, require on these points, as to the nature of God.

In the first place, God is not to be treated as an exception to all metaphysical principles, invoked to save their collapse. God is their chief exemplification. The final summary can only be expressed in terms of a group of antitheses, whose apparent self-contradiction depend on neglect of the diverse categories of existence. In each antithesis there is a shift of meaning which converts the opposition into a contrast.

> *It is as true to say that God is permanent and the World fluent, as that the World is permanent and God is fluent.*

> *It is as true to say that God is one and the World many, as the world is one and God many.*

> *It is as true to say that, in comparison with the World, God is actual eminently, as that, in comparison with God, the World is actual eminently.*

> *It is as true to say that the World is immanent in God, as that God is immanent in the World.*

> *It is as true to say that God transcends the World, as that the World transcends God.*

> *It is as true to say that God creates the World, as that the World creates God.*

Thus God is to be conceived as one and as many in the converse sense in which the World is to be conceived as many and as one. The theme of Cosmology, which is the basis of all religion, is the story of the dynamic effort of the World passing into everlasting unity, and of the static majesty of God's vision, accomplishing its purpose of completion by absorption of the World's multiplicity of effort.

Thus the universe is to be conceived as attaining the active self-expression of its own variety of opposites—of its own freedom and its own necessity, of its own multiplicity and its own unity, of its own imperfection and its own perfection. All the "opposites" are elements in the nature of things, and are incorrigibly there. The concept of "God" is the way in which we understand this incredible fact—that what cannot be, yet is.

*God is the great companion—the fellow-sufferer who understands.*

# V

## Creation—A Continuous Process

It was a mistake, as the Hebrews tried, to conceive of God as creating the world from the outside, at one go. An all-foreseeing Creator, who could have made the world as we find it now what could we think of such a being? Foreseeing everything and yet putting into it all sorts of imperfections, to redeem which it was necessary to send his only son into the world to suffer torture and hideous death; outrageous ideas. The Hellenic religion was a better approach; the Greeks conceived of creation as going on everywhere all the time *within* the universe; and I also think they were happier in their conception of supernatural beings impersonating those various forces, some good, others bad; for both sorts of forces *are* present, whether we assign personality to them or not. There is a general tendency in the universe to produce worthwhile things, and moments come when we can work with it and it can work through us. But that tendency in the universe to produce worthwhile things is by no means omnipotent. Other forces work against it.

God *is in* the universe, or nowhere, creating continually in us and around us. This creative principle is everywhere, in animate and so-called inanimate matter, in the ether, water, earth, human hearts. But this creation is a continuing process, and "the process is itself the actuality," since no sooner do you arrive than you start on a fresh journey. Insofar as we partake of this creative process do we partake of the divine, of God, and that participation is our immortality, reducing the question of whether our individuality survives death of the body to the estate of an irrelevancy. Our true destiny as cocreator in the universe is our dignity and our grandeur.

# The Need for Transcendence in the Postmodern World

## Vaclav Havel

*In this postmodern world, cultural conflicts are becoming more danger-ous than any time in history. A new model of coexistence is needed, based on man's transcending himself. This address was delivered in Independence Hall, Philadelphia, July 4, 1994, by the President of the Czech Republic from 1993 to 2003.*

There are thinkers who claim that, if the modern age began with the discovery of America, it also ended in America. This is said to have occurred in the year 1969, when America sent the first men to the moon. From this historical moment, they say, a new age in the life of humanity can be dated.

I think there are good reasons for suggesting that the modern age has ended. Today, many things indicate that we are going thorough a transitional period, when it seems that something is on the way out and something else is painfully being born. It is as if something were crumbling, decaying, and exhausting itself, while something else, still indistinct, were arising from the rubble.

Periods of history when values undergo a fundamental shift are certainly not unprecedented. This happened in the Hellenistic peri-od, when from the ruins of the classical world the Middle Ages were

106

gradually born. It happened during the Renaissance, which opened the way to the modern era. The distinguishing features of such transitional periods are a mixing and blending of cultures and a plurality or parallelism of intellectual and spiritual worlds. These are periods when all consistent value systems collapse, when cultures distant in time and space are discovered or rediscovered. They are periods when there is a tendency to quote, to imitate, and to amplify, rather than to state with authority or integrate. New meaning is gradually born from the encounter, or the intersection, of many different elements.

Today, this state of mind or of the human world is called postmodernism. For me, a symbol of that state is a Bedouin mounted on a camel and clad in traditional robes under which he is wearing jeans, with a transistor radio in his hands and an ad for Coca-Cola on the camel's back. I am not ridiculing this, nor am I shedding an intellectual tear over the commercial expansion of the West that destroys alien cultures. I see it rather as a typical expression of this multicultural era, a signal that an amalgamation of cultures is taking place. I see it as proof that something is happening, something is being born, that we are in a phase when one age is succeeding another, when everything is possible. Yes, everything is possible, because our civilization does not have its own unified style, its own spirit, its own aesthetic.

# I
# Science and Modern Civilization

This is related to the crisis, or to the transformation, of science as the basis of the modern conception of the world.

The dizzying development of this science, with its unconditional faith in objective reality and its complete dependency on general and rationally knowable laws, led to the birth of modern technological civilization. It is the first civilization in the history of the human race that spans the entire globe and firmly binds together all human societies, submitting them to a common global destiny. It was this science that enabled man, for the first time, to see Earth from space with his own eyes; that is, to see it as another star in the sky.

At the same time, however, the relationship to the world that the modern science fostered and shaped now appears to have exhausted its potential. It is increasingly clear that, strangely, the relationship is missing something. It fails to connect with the most intrinsic nature of reality and with natural human experience. It is now more of a source of disintegration and doubt than a source of integration and meaning. It produces what amounts to a state of schizophrenia: Man as an observer is becoming completely alienated from himself as a being.

Classical modern science described only the surface of things, a single dimension of reality. And the more dogmatically science treated it as the only dimension, as the very essence of reality, the more misleading it became. Today, for instance, we may know immeasurably more about the universe than our ancestors did, and yet, it increasingly seems they knew something more essential about it than we do, something that escapes us. The same thing is true of nature and of ourselves. The more thoroughly all our organs and their functions, their internal structure, and the biochemical reactions that take place within them are described, the more we seem to fail to grasp the spirit, purpose, and meaning of the system that they create together and that we experience as our unique "self".

And thus today we find ourselves in a paradoxical situation. We enjoy all the achievements of modern civilization that have made our physical existence on this earth easier so in many important ways. Yet we do not know exactly what to do with ourselves, where to turn. The world of our experiences seems chaotic, disconnected, confusing. There appear to be no integrating forces, no unified meaning, no true inner understanding of phenomena in our experience of the world. Experts can explain anything in the objective world to us, yet we understand our own lives less and less. In short, we live in the postmodern world, where everything is possible and almost nothing is certain.

# II
# When Nothing is Certain

This state of affairs has its social and political consequences. The single planetary civilization to which we all belong confronts us with global challenges. We stand helpless before them because our civilization has essentially globalized only the surfaces of our lives. But our inner self continues to have a life of its own. And the fewer answers the era of rational knowledge provides to the basic questions of human Being, the more deeply it would seem that people, behind its back as it were, cling to the ancient certainties of their tribe. Because of this, individual cultures, increasingly lumped together by contemporary civilization, are realizing with new urgency their own inner autonomy and the inner differences of others.

Cultural conflicts are increasing and are understandably more dangerous today than at any other time in history. The end of the era of rationalism has been catastrophic. Armed with the same supermodern weapons, often from the same suppliers, and followed by television cameras, the members of various tribal cults are at war with one another. By day, we work with statistics; in the evening, we consult astrologers and frighten ourselves with thrillers about vampires. The abyss between rational and the spiritual, the external and the internal, the objective and the subjective, the technical and the moral, the universal and the unique, constantly grows deeper.

Politicians are rightly worried by the problem of finding the key to ensure the survival of a civilization that is global and at the same time clearly multicultural. How can generally respected mechanisms of peaceful coexistence be set up, and on what set of principles are they to be established?

These questions have been highlighted with particular urgency by the two most important political events in the second half of the twentieth century: the collapse of colonial hegemony and the fall of communism. The artificial world order of the past decades has collapsed, and a new, more just order has not yet emerged. The central political task of the final years of this century, then, is the creation of a new model of coexistence among the various cultures, peoples, races, and religious spheres within a single interconnected civilization. This task is all the more urgent because other threats to contemporary humanity brought about by one-dimensional development of civilization are growing more serious all the time.

Many believe this task can be accomplished through technical means. That is, they believe it can be accomplished through the intervention of new organizational, political, and diplomatic instruments. Yes, it is clearly necessary to invent organizational structures appropriate to the present multicultural age. But such efforts are doomed to failure if they do not grow out of something deeper, out of generally held values.

This, too, is well known. And in searching for the most natural source for the creation of a new world order, we usually look to an area that is the traditional foundation of modern justice and a great achievement of the modern age: to a set of values that—among other things—were first declared in this building (Independence Hall). I am referring to respect for the unique human being and his or her liberties and inalienable rights and to the principle that all power derives from the people. I am, in short, referring to the fundamental ideas of modern democracy.

What I am about to say may sound provocative, but I feel more and more strongly that even these ideas are not enough, that we must go farther and deeper. The point is that the solution they offer is still, as it were, modern, derived from the climate of the Enlightenment and from a view of man and his relation to the world that has been characteristic of the Euro-American sphere for the last two centuries. Today, however, we are in a different place and facing a different situation, one to which classical modern solutions in themselves do not give a satisfactory response. After all, the very principle of inalienable human rights, conferred on man by the Creator, grew out of the typically modern notion that man—as a being capable of knowing nature and the world—was the pinnacle of creation and lord of the world,

This modern anthropocentrism inevitably meant that He who allegedly endowed man with his inalienable rights began to disappear from the world: He was so far beyond the grasp of modern science that he was gradually pushed into a sphere of privacy of sorts, if not directly into a sphere of private fancy—that is, to a place where public obligations no longer apply. The existence of a higher authority than man himself simply began to get in the way of human aspirations.

## III
## Two Transcendent Ideas

The idea of human rights and freedoms must be an integral part of any meaningful world order. Yet, I think it must be anchored in a different place, and in a different way, than has been the case so far. If it is to be more than just a slogan mocked by half the world, it cannot be expressed in the language of a departing era, and it must not be mere froth floating on the subsiding waters of faith in a purely scientific relationship to the world.

Paradoxically, inspiration for the renewal of this lost integrity can once again be found in science, in a science that is new—let us say postmodern—a science producing ideas that in a certain sense allow it to transcend its own limits. I will give two examples:

The first is the Anthropic Cosmological Principle. Its authors and adherents have pointed out that from the countless possible courses of its evolution the universe took the only one that enabled life to emerge. This is not yet proof that the aim of the universe has always been that it should one day see itself through our eyes. But how else can this matter be explained?

I think the Anthropic Cosmological Principle brings to us an idea perhaps as old as humanity itself: that we are not at all just an accidental anomaly, the microscopic caprice of a tine particle whirling in the endless depth of the universe. Instead, we are mysteriously connected to the entire universe, we are mirrored in it, just as the entire evolution of the universe is mirrored in us.

Until recently, it might have seemed that we were an unhappy bit of mildew on a heavenly body whirling in space among many that have no mildew on them at all. This was something that classical science could explain. Yet, the moment it begins to appear that we are deeply connected to the entire universe, science reaches the outer limits of its powers. Because it is founded on the search for universal laws, it cannot deal with singularity, that is, with uniqueness. The universe is a unique event and a unique story, and so far we are the unique point of that story. But unique events and stories are the domain of poetry, not science. With the formulation of the Anthropic Cosmological Principle, science has found itself on the border between formula and story, between science and myth. In that, however, science has paradoxically returned, in a roundabout way, to man, and offers him—in new clothing—his lost integrity. It does so by anchoring him once more in the cosmos.

The second example is the Gaia Hypothesis. This theory brings together proof that the dense network of mutual interactions between the organic and inorganic portions of the earth's surface form a single system, a kind of mega-organism, a living planet—Gaia—named after an ancient goddess who is recognizable as an archetype of the Earth Mother in perhaps all religions. According to the Gaia Hypothesis, we are parts of a greater whole. If we endanger her, she will dispense with us in the interest of a higher value—that is, life itself.

# IV
## Toward Self-Transcendence

What makes the Anthropic Principle and the Gaia Hypothesis so inspiring? One simple thing: Both remind us, in modern language, of what we have long suspected, of what we have long projected into our forgotten myths and perhaps what has always lain dormant within us as archetypes. That is, the awareness of our being anchored in the earth and the universe, the awareness that we are not here alone nor for ourselves alone, but that we are an integral part of higher, mysterious entities against whom it is not advisable to blaspheme. This forgotten awareness is encoded in all religions. All cultures anticipate it in various forms. It is one of the things that form the basis of man's understanding of himself, of his place in the world, and ultimately of the world as such.

A modern philosopher once said: "Only a God can save us now."

Yes, the only real hope of people today is probably a renewal of our certainty that we are rooted in the earth and, at the same time, in the cosmos. This awareness endows us with the capacity for self-transcendence. Politicians at international forums may reiterate a thousand times that the basis of the new world order must be universal respects for human rights, but it will mean nothing as long as this imperative does not derive from the respect of the miracle of Being, the miracle of the universe, the miracle of nature, the miracle of our own existence. Only someone who submits to the authority of the universal order and of creation, who values the right to be a part of it and a participant in it, can genuinely value himself and his neighbors, and thus honor their rights as well.

It logically follows that, in today's multicultural world, the truly reliable path to coexistence, to peaceful coexistence and creative cooperation, must start from what is at the root of all cultures and what lies infinitely deeper in human hearts and minds than political opinion, convictions, antipathies, or sympathies—it must be rooted in self-transcendence:

- Transcendence as a hand reached out to those close to us, to foreigners, to the human community, to all living creatures, to nature, to the universe.

- Transcendence as a deeply and joyously experienced need to be in harmony even with what we ourselves are not, what we do not understand, what seems distant from us in time and space, but with which we are nevertheless mysteriously linked because, together with us, all this constitutes a single world.

- Transcendence as the only real alternative to extinction.

The Declaration of Independence states that the Creator gave man the right to liberty. It seems man can realize that liberty only if he does not forget the One who endowed him with it.

www.ingramcontent.com/pod-product-compliance
Lightning Source LLC
Chambersburg PA
CBHW051812040426
42446CB00007B/631